GETTING IT RIGHT

Food Processor Recipes

D0608725

GETTING IT RIGHT

Food Processor Recipes

by Daphne Metland

foulsham

LONDON • NEW YORK • TORONTO • SYDNEY

foulsham
Yeovil Road, Slough, Berkshire, SL1 4JH

These recipes represent a small selection from:
New Recipes for Your Food Processor

ISBN 0-572-01927-0

Printed in Great Britain by Cox & Wyman Ltd., Reading.

CONTENTS

Introduction 6

How to Use your Food Processor 7

Ten Food Processor Tips 15

The Recipes 16

Soups and Starters 17

Salads and Salad Dressings 29

Pastry 39

Main Meals 59

Sauces and Stuffings 79

Vegetables 87

Desserts 97

Cakes, Biscuits and Yeast Cookery 103

Preserves 117

Index 123

INTRODUCTION

Food processors must represent the greatest change in food preparation appliances since the original Heath Robinson style machines that peeled apples and boiled eggs by means of string and pulleys, amazed Victorian cooks, and gave many a scullery maid cause to be thankful to modern science.

Food processors are powerful, hard-working machines that can chop, purée, slice, shred and mix most foods in seconds. They take most of the hard work out of cooking, leaving the enjoyable parts for the cook to do.

Food processors were introduced about ten years ago, and over the past decade a wide variety of different shapes and sizes of food processor, with many different attachments, have come onto the market. Techniques vary little from machine to machine, but do make the effort to read the instruction booklet thoroughly when first using your food processor. The power of the machine does influence how quickly food is processed, but since overprocessing is the most common problem I have quoted minimum processing times in the recipes. Experience will soon guide you in judging the correct time for your particular machine.

We have included basic step-by-step recipes in most sections of this book to help you get the best from your food processor. Use the skills learnt from these guides in the recipes which follow. Once you become confident with the things that your processor can do, try experimenting with your own variations.

It is well worth leaving a food processor out on the worktop ready for instant use. Any machine hidden away in a cupboard tends to stay there. However, worktop space is valuable and any gadget or machine in my small kitchen has to earn the space it takes up. My food processor has pride of place; I hope yours will too.

HOW TO USE YOUR FOOD PROCESSOR

The Right Timing

The power of a food processor means that it is all too easy to overprocess foods, especially when using the metal blade. Onions can be nicely chopped in three seconds and puréed in five, and meat can be minced in eight seconds and ground to a paste in twelve. It is very important to keep an eye on the food in the processor and to stop and check the condition of the food during the processing time. Never leave the machine unattended and always err on the side of undertiming rather than overtiming. It is easy to switch on again for an extra second or two. All the recipes in this book give approximate timing achieved simply by counting slowly when processing. Machines do vary slightly in the time they take to process foods, depending on how powerful they are and the size of the bowl. Recipes therefore give the approximate time to process and a description of what the food should look like, for example, 'process for ten seconds until finely chopped'.

Some machines have a pulse button that allows the motor to be switched on and off very quickly and this is a useful way of getting the desired result. Even without a pulse button it is quite quick and easy to turn the machine on and off two or three times to be sure of getting just the right texture.

The Right Load

Avoid overloading the machine. The bowl capacity limits the amount of food that can be processed at any one time and too much food will cause uneven processing. This is noticeable as large lumps of food sitting on top of the processed food. Process large quantities of food in batches, and remove the finished food to a bowl while the next load is being processed. The capacity of machines varies, but as a rough guide most will cope with between 8 oz/225 grams and 12 oz/340 grams of meat, or a three-egg victoria sandwich mixture or up to 1 lb/450 grams of bread dough. Cake mixtures, pâtés and the like will need scraping down during processing, and this can usually be done when other ingredients are being added.

The Right Order

Minimise washing up by preparing foods in the right order. Make up the foods which will cause the least mess first; for instance for a quiche prepare the pastry first and then the filling so there is no need to wash up after the pastry is made. Often just scraping the bowl with a spatula is sufficient. All the recipes in this book have been written with this in mind so it is usually only necessary to wash the bowl and attachments at the end of the recipes. There are exceptions, of course, particularly with foods such as beetroot which will stain everything it comes into contact with. Sometimes the remaining fragments of food actually enhance the next step of the recipe, for instance when making a salad dressing after slicing the vegetables to go in the salad.

Safety

The blades and discs on any processor are very sharp; they have to be to do the job. It is important to observe the following points when using your machine.

*** Do not touch the blades or discs while they are still revolving. All food processors need the lid in place to work, but it can take a few seconds for the blades to stop turning once the machine is turned off.

*** Never reach in and pick up the blade or disc by the sharp cutting edge. Instead, lift the bowl off the motor base, so loosening the attachment, and pick up the blade carefully by the plastic centre piece or the discs by the rim.

*** Never leave blades or discs in the washing up bowl. Stand them on the worktop where they can be easily seen until you are ready to wash up.

*** Store the blades safely.

Cleaning

Bowls and lids can be washed in the sink, and some are dishwasher proof, but do check in the instruction booklet. Blades and discs need to be washed with a small brush, preferably under running water. A small bottle brush will help keep the inside of the plastic centre, where it fits onto the motor base, clean. Dry all parts well and leave the lid off when re-assembling to allow air to circulate. The motor base should never be immersed in water. Unplug and wipe clean with a barely damp cloth.

Storage

If possible keep your processor out on the worktop, but store the blades and discs safely – perhaps in a wall cupboard if there are children in the house. Some companies make storage racks for the various attachments for their machines. Do not store in a general cutlery drawer!

Using the Attachments

All food processors have a metal blade, a slicing disc and a grating disc. These three attachments are mentioned in the recipes in this book. Many also have plastic blades and other discs. Do refer to the instruction booklet supplied with your machine to check which is the most suitable for which job. Here is a short guide to the uses of the basic attachments. Try them out before you start on an actual recipe so you know how they work.

METAL BLADE
This is the most versatile of the fitments. It is used for chopping cooked and uncooked meats, fish and poultry, and for reducing these to a purée or paste. Vegetables such as onions, carrots, potatoes and fruits can be chopped and puréed. It also makes breadcrumbs, sauces and can be used for chopping and grinding nuts, and for cake, bread and biscuit mixtures. Some processors also have a plastic blade that is designed for these last few items.

SLICING DISC
Hard vegetables and fruits such as cabbage, raw potatoes, carrots, leeks, apples and pears will all slice through the slicing disc. Foods should be

trimmed to fit the feed tube and held in place with the pusher, not the fingers! Small foods such as carrots and leeks will need to be stacked in the feed tube so that they do not fall over while being processed as this will change the finished shape of the food. Some foods will need processing in batches as the bowl will quickly fill with sliced food.

Tinned meats can be sliced if they are chilled in the refrigerator for an hour or so before use. Take care not to push down too hard with the pusher. It is also possible to thinly slice raw meats but only if still partly frozen. Even foods such as firm strawberries, peaches, tomatoes and cooked potatoes can be sliced with care.

Remember that the way you stack the food in the feed tube determines the shape of the finished slices. Apple halves positioned horizontally will make crescent-shaped slices, while placed vertically will make semicircular slices. Long foods such as bananas, carrots or courgettes can be sliced into circles or long strips as you prefer. Use the pusher as a guide for measuring the correct size of food to go through the feed tube.

Sometimes pieces of food catch on the slicing or grating discs and this is quite normal. If a great deal of food catches on the discs, however, the food was probably not loaded correctly in the feed tube.

GRATING DISC
The grating disc will cope with most hard vegetables as well as cheeses and chocolate. It is ideal for salad foods, and ingredients such as carrots, beetroot, celeriac and cucumber can all be grated successfully. Many families find it convenient to grate enough cheese for several days

11

and store it in a plastic box in the refrigerator so that it is always ready for packed lunches and snacks.

WHISKS

Some processors have whisk attachments, but it is important to remember that the amount of air that can be introduced into foods such as egg whites and cream is limited by the fact that a processor has a lid. The whisking is generally sufficient for mousses but not really suitable for meringues or for cream stiff enough to pipe, although some of the newer whisk attachments give quite good results. Check in the instruction leaflet about the suitability of the whisk attachment for various dishes. Throughout this book, recipes suggest that egg whites are whisked by hand, but it is possible to fold in egg whites by adding them to the processsor and operating the machine for 2 to 3 seconds only.

OTHER ATTACHMENTS

Many companies offer other discs and attachments for food processors as optional extras. Their uses are not as universal as those mentioned above, but the chipping disc may well be popular with families keen on chips, and it can also be used to make vegetable sticks for dips and parties. Some of the larger processors also have juice extractors and pasta makers that fit to the motor base.

Noise

Some machines are undoubtedly noisier than others, but noise can be minimised by ensuring that the machine is always on a firm worktop and by not overloading it. Some foods, particularly hard ones like nuts and chocolate, will make a great deal of noise while being processed. Overloading may also cause excessive vibration, and some machines do tend to 'walk' if overloaded.

Exceptions to the Rule

While food processors can cope with most foods, there are some that should not be prepared in the processor. Whole grains and coffee beans are not generally recommended, and some manufacturers do not recommend crushing ice in their machines. Others do, so again this is something to check in the instruction booklet. I personally find that potatoes do not mash very well in the processor as they tend to be overworked, even in a few seconds. Egg whites for meringues and cream for piping are the other two foods I would not recommend.

Baby Foods

A processor makes light work of puréeing foods for babies. Simply place the food in the processor, moisten with a little milk or stock and process for a few seconds. Rice, pasta, potatoes, meat, chicken, vegetables and fish all process well, and as the baby progresses onto less smooth foods, simply process for a shorter period. It is often worthwhile preparing a reasonable quantity of food for the baby and then freezing it in ice cube trays, so that just the right amount can be removed from the freezer at any one time.

13

Waste Not Want Not

A processor can help make economies in the kitchen. Small quantities of leftover food can be sliced, grated or chopped finely and added to a sauce to make it go further. Garnishes to dress up a dish can be made quickly and easily, and even a few winter vegetables can be turned into a quick soup. For anyone with a freezer, foods bought cheaply at the height of the season can be quickly puréed or sliced and frozen ready for use later in the year.

TEN FOOD PROCESSOR TIPS

1. Save all the oddments of cheese that are usually thrown away, and grate them in the processor. Freeze in a plastic bag or tub and use, straight from the freezer, to add to sauces and toppings.
2. Cut oranges, lemons and limes in half and slice through the slicing disc. Freeze and have ready to add to drinks or use as a garnish.
3. For extra-quick soups, chop all the vegetables finely in the processor, mix with the stock and cook for ten minutes, then purée.
4. Make bread dough in the processor and prove overnight in the fridge. Bake fresh in the morning.
5. Try home made crisps: thinly slice potatoes, and pat the slices dry. Deep fry and drain well. Sprinkle with salt before serving.
6. Use leftover meat or poultry to make tasty sandwich fillings. Mix the meat with butter and seasoning and purée well.
7. When making cakes, add the cherries or fruit at the end and process for just 2 to 3 seconds to avoid them being cut into very small pieces.
8. Soups can be puréed quickly by draining off most of the liquid and puréeing the remaining vegetables in the processor. Add the liquid to the vegetables back in the pan and reheat.
9. Remember to trim meat well as gristle and fat will process but remain hard when cooked. Even stewing steak is suitable for hamburgers as long as it is well trimmed.
10. Make Royal icing that is glossy and easy to pipe by mixing the egg white in the processor with the metal blade and then adding the icing sugar in batches.

THE RECIPES

All the recipes in this book are designed to serve four, unless otherwise specified.

All spoon measurements are level.

All the recipes give approximate processing times, achieved simply by counting slowly when processing, followed by a description of what the food should look like. Machines do vary slightly in the time they take to process foods, so check the condition of the food during the processing time and adjust if necessary to suit your own machine.

The following symbols are used at the beginning of the recipes.

 Suitable for freezing for the time specified. N.B. Recipes without this symbol are not suitable for freezing.

 Use the metal blade.

 Use the slicing disc.

 Use the grating disc.

SOUPS AND STARTERS

Deliciously warming as winter starters, or a satisfying meal when served with bread and cheese, soups are extremely versatile. They are also very quick and easy to make in the processor, since all the fiddly and time-consuming chopping and slicing is done for you. For smooth, creamy soups, purée the cooked soup in the processor.

Pâtés can be served as a starter, or with salad as a lunch-time dish. Food processors are great for making pâté. Adjust the processing time to give rough or smooth pâté and use different cuts of pork, poultry or veal.

Other starter dishes such as Hummus and Avocado and Tuna Mousse are also prepared with ease in the processor.

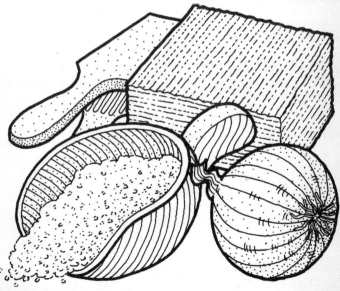

Leek and Potato Soup

The following recipe for Leek and Potato Soup is a simple step-by-step guide for the preparation of soup in the processor. Once you are happy with the basic technique, experiment with other vegetables. A selection of recipes for you to try is given in this section.

INGREDIENTS

	Imperial	Metric	American
Leeks	3	3	3
Potatoes	3	3	3
Celery	1 stick	1 stick	1 stick
Butter	1 oz	25 g	2 tbsp
Chicken stock	1 pt	600 ml	2½ cups
Salt and freshly ground black pepper			
Single (light) cream	¼ pt	150 ml	⅔ cup

1. Fit the SLICING DISC. Wash the leeks, and trim them to fit the feed tube. Slice through the slicing disc. Remove from the bowl.
2. Peel the potatoes and trim to fit the feed tube. Slice through the slicing disc.
3. Wash and trim the celery, and slice.
4. Place all the vegetables in a large pan, and cook in a little butter for 5 minutes until the vegetables are slightly softened. Add the stock and season. Cook for 15–20 minutes.
5. Fit the METAL BLADE. Add the hot soup. This may need to be done in two batches in some processors. Alternatively, pour off most of the stock, and purée the vegetables, then mix the stock and vegetable purée in the pan. Add the cream and heat but do not boil.
6. The thickened soup can be served hot or cold, but is best with a little cream or milk stirred in.

French Onion Soup

✻ 2 months

INGREDIENTS	Imperial	Metric	American
Onions	*1 lb*	*450 g*	*1 lb*
Butter	*2 oz*	*50 g*	*¼ cup*
Oil	*1 tbsp*	*1 tbsp*	*1 tbsp*
Beef stock	*2 pt*	*1.1 l*	*5 cups*
Potatoes	*2 medium*	*2 medium*	*2 medium*
Cheese	*2 oz*	*50 g*	*2 oz*
French mustard	*½ tsp*	*½ tsp*	*½ tsp*
Mixed herbs	*½ tsp*	*½ tsp*	*½ tsp*
Butter	*½ tsp*	*½ tsp*	*½ tsp*
Salt and freshly ground black pepper			
French bread	*½ loaf*	*½ loaf*	*½ loaf*

Use the SLICING DISC. Peel the onions, trim and cut to fit the feed tube. Slice. Fry gently in the butter and oil until golden brown. Add the stock. Peel the potatoes and slice through the feed tube. Add to the stock. Simmer for 15 minutes.

Fit the METAL BLADE. Drop the roughly chopped cheese onto the blade. Combine the mustard, herbs, butter, and salt and pepper to taste by processing for 5 seconds. Cut the French loaf into thick slices and spread each one with some of the mixture. Either toast under the grill and serve with the soup, or put the cheese-topped bread in a large oven-proof casserole, pour the soup on top and heat in a hot oven 400°F/200°C/Gas mark 6 for about 10 minutes until golden brown.

TO FREEZE
Freeze without the bread and cheese mixture.

Winter Vegetable Soup

❄ 3 months

INGREDIENTS	Imperial	Metric	American
Onion	1	1	1
Garlic	1 clove	1 clove	1 clove
Potato	1	1	1
Carrot	1	1	1
Leek	1	1	1
Celery	1 stick	1 stick	1 stick
Oil	1 tbsp	1 tbsp	1 tbsp
Sherry	3 tbsp	3 tbsp	3 tbsp
Chicken stock	1½ pt	850 ml	3¾ cups
Mixed herbs	1 tsp	1 tsp	1 tsp
Salt and freshly ground			
black pepper			

Use the METAL BLADE. Peel the onion and the garlic clove and cut each into 4 pieces. Process for 3 seconds until chopped or use the pulse button 2 or 3 times until the correct fineness is obtained. Remove. Peel the potato and cut into 4. Peel and trim the carrot and cut into 4. Wash and trim the leek and cut into 4. Process together for 3 seconds until chopped. Remove. Wash and trim the celery and cut into 4. Process for 3 seconds. Heat the oil in a large pan, gently sweat the onion and garlic for 3–4 minutes without browning. Add the leek, potato and carrot, and stir well, then add the celery and stir. Add the sherry and stir, then pour in the stock. Add the herbs and season to taste. Bring to the boil, then simmer gently for 20 minutes.

Serve hot with grated cheese or croûtons. Makes a good light lunch.

Velvety Carrot Soup

3 months

INGREDIENTS	Imperial	Metric	American
Onion	1	1	1
Garlic	1 clove	1 clove	1 clove
Carrots	1 lb	450 g	1 lb
Oil	1 tbsp	1 tbsp	1 tbsp
Chicken stock	1 pt	600 ml	2½ cups
Sugar	¼ tsp	¼ tsp	¼ tsp
Salt and freshly ground black pepper			
Single (light) cream	¼ pt	150 ml	⅔ cup

Use the METAL BLADE. Peel the onion and cut into 4. Peel the garlic clove and cut into 4. Process for 3–4 seconds (or use the pulse button 3 or 4 times) until finely chopped.

Fit the SLICING DISC. Scrub or peel the carrots, trim, then slice. Heat the oil in a large pan, sweat the onion and garlic gently for 3–4 minutes until soft. Add the sliced carrots and stir, then pour in the stock and sugar and season to taste. Cook for 15 minutes until the carrots are soft.

Fit the METAL BLADE. Purée the soup in 2 batches, return to the pan and add the cream. Heat through thoroughly, but do not allow to boil.

Serve hot with croûtons.

TO FREEZE
Cool and pour into a plastic box. Thaw at room temperature for 3–4 hours. Reheat thoroughly in a saucepan.
NOTE: These instructions also apply to Winter Vegetable Soup.

Pâté

INGREDIENTS	Imperial	Metric	American
Onion	1	1	1
Garlic	1 clove	1 clove	1 clove
Streaky bacon	4 oz	100 g	¼ lb
Belly of pork	8 oz	225 g	½ lb
Liver	8 oz	225 g	½ lb
Butter	1 oz	25 g	2 tbsp
Single (light) cream	2 tbsp	2 tbsp	2 tbsp
Ground mace	½ tsp	½ tsp	½ tsp
Salt and freshly ground black pepper			

1. Fit the METAL BLADE. Cut the onion into quarters, and cut the garlic into 3. Process for 3–5 seconds.
2. The chopped onions should be even, without being watery. Process the onions in several short bursts at first, until you are sure just how long they take in your processor.
3. Derind and chop the bacon. Derind and remove eyes from the pork, cut each slice into 4. Other types of meat, such a veal, poultry or game may be used, or leaner cuts of pork, according to taste.
4. Process the bacon and pork together for 10–15 seconds, then add the liver and process until it is evenly incorporated.
5. Add the butter, cut into pieces, and the cream and seasoning.
6. The finished pâté can be turned into a dish lined with bacon.

Chicken and Mushroom Pâté

2 months   Serves 6

INGREDIENTS	Imperial	Metric	American
Mushrooms	*4 oz*	*100 g*	*¼ lb*
Onion	*1 small*	*1 small*	*1 small*
Butter	*2 oz*	*50 g*	*¼ cup*
Chicken livers	*8 oz*	*225 g*	*½ lb*
Sherry	*1 tbsp*	*1 tbsp*	*1 tbsp*
Double (heavy) cream	*2 tbsp*	*2 tbsp*	*2 tbsp*
Butter	*½ oz*	*15 g*	*1 tbsp*
Cooked chicken	*4 oz*	*100 g*	*¼ lb*

Use the SLICING DISC. Wipe the mushrooms and slice through the slicing disc. Remove.

Fit the METAL BLADE. Trim and peel the onion, cut it into 4 and process for 3–4 seconds until finely chopped. Fry in half the butter until soft. Add the chicken livers and fry for 10 minutes until just cooked. Add the sherry and stir well, then add the cream and the remaining butter. Cut the cooked chicken into pieces and process for 3–4 seconds until finely chopped. Add the chicken liver mixture and process for 7 seconds. Spread the ½ oz/15 g butter on the base of a ½ lb/225 g loaf tin and arrange half the mushrooms on the base. Spread half the pâté on top and then arrange the remaining mushrooms on top. Finish with another layer of pâté. Cover with foil and place in a baking dish half full of water. Bake at 375°F/190°C/Gas mark 5 for 30 minutes. Cool in the tin, then put weights on top (or use tins of food) and chill overnight. Turn out and cut into slices to serve. This soft-textured pâté must be well chilled to slice. Freeze in slices, interleaved with foil. Place in polythene bag. Thaw for 2-3 hours.

Smoked Mackerel Pâté

 3 months

INGREDIENTS	Imperial	Metric	American
Lemon	1	1	1
Smoked mackerel	8 oz	225 g	½ lb
Butter	2 oz	50 g	¼ cup
Ground mace	½ tsp	½ tsp	½ tsp
Double (heavy) cream	1 tbsp	1 tbsp	1 tbsp
Freshly ground black pepper			

Use the SLICING DISC. Cut the lemon in half lengthways. Slice one half through the slicing disc. Remove from the bowl.

Fit the METAL BLADE. Remove the skin from the fish and cut up roughly. Place in the processor and process for 7–8 seconds until well flaked. Cut the butter into 4–6 pieces and, with the motor running, drop the pieces one by one through the feed tube until they are fully mixed in. Stop the machine, add the mace, the cream, the juice of the remaining half of the lemon, and black pepper to taste and mix for 3–4 seconds.

Place the pâté in a serving dish and arrange the lemon slices on top. Chill for one hour before serving.

Serve cold as a starter with toast or biscuits.

TO FREEZE
Freeze in small portions or individual dishes covered with clingfilm. Thaw at room temperature for 3–4 hours.

Bacon and Sweetcorn Chowder

Serves 4–6

INGREDIENTS	Imperial	Metric	American
Onion	*1 large*	*1 large*	*1 large*
Oil	*1 tbsp*	*1 tbsp*	*1 tbsp*
Bacon	*6 oz*	*175 g*	*6 oz*
Celery	*1 stick*	*1 stick*	*1 stick*
Green pepper	*1 small*	*1 small*	*1 small*
Potato	*1 med*	*1 med*	*1 med*
Sherry	*1 tbsp*	*1 tbsp*	*1 tbsp*
Chicken stock	*1 pt*	*600 ml*	*2½ cups*
Sweetcorn (frozen or canned)	*8 oz*	*225 g*	*½ lb*
Milk	*½ pt*	*300 ml*	*1¼ cups*
Salt and freshly ground black pepper			

Use the METAL BLADE. Peel and trim the onion, cut into 4 and place in the processor bowl. Process in 2 or 3 short bursts or use the pulse button until evenly chopped. Heat the oil in a large pan. Fry the onion for 5 minutes. Chop the bacon in the processor for 4–5 seconds and then fry with the onion. Wash the celery and cut into 4, trim and deseed the pepper and cut into 4. Place both in the processor and process in 3 short bursts until evenly chopped. Add to the pan. Peel and quarter the potato, process for 3 seconds until evenly chopped. Add to the pan. Pour in the sherry. Stir well. (There will be a cloud of steam and a loud sizzling.) Add the stock. Bring to the boil, simmer for 10–15 minutes until the vegetables are tender. Add the sweetcorn, cook gently for a further 10

25

minutes then stir in the milk and season
generously. Cook for a further 5 minutes but do
not allow to boil.

Serve hot. Makes a complete meal if served
with wholemeal or French bread and butter.

NOTE
Do not freeze.

Avocado and Tuna Mousse

INGREDIENTS	Imperial	Metric	American
Avocado pear	1	1	1
Canned tuna fish	1 small can	1 small can	1 small can
Natural yoghurt	2 tbsp	2 tbsp	2 tbsp
Tabasco sauce	1 tsp	1 tsp	1 tsp
Lemon juice	1 tsp	1 tsp	1 tsp
Freshly ground black pepper			

Use the METAL BLADE. Cut the avocado in half,
remove the stone and peel each half. Cut it into 8
pieces in total and place in the processor. Process
for 10 seconds. It may be necessary to scrape down
the sides of the bowl half-way through. Add the
drained tuna fish, the yoghurt, tabasco sauce and
lemon juice. Process for a further 10 seconds.
Taste and add extra tabasco if liked and freshly
ground black pepper to taste. Pile into a dish and
chill before serving.

Serve as a starter with toast or bread, or as a
party dip.

NOTE
Do not freeze.

Hummus

INGREDIENTS	Imperial	Metric	American
Chick peas	4 oz	100 g	¼ lb
Onion	1	1	1
Garlic	2 cloves	2 cloves	2 cloves
Natural yoghurt	¼ pt	150 ml	⅔ cup
Lemon juice	2 tsp	2 tsp	2 tsp
Oil	1 tbsp	1 tbsp	1 tbsp
Cumin	½ tsp	½ tsp	½ tsp
Salt			

Use the METAL BLADE. Soak the chick peas
overnight. Drain and place in a pan with sufficient
water to cover. Peel and trim the onion, chop in
the processor for 3–4 seconds and add to the chick
peas. Peel and trim the garlic, chop in the
processor for 3–4 seconds and add to the chick
peas. Bring to the boil and simmer for about an
hour until tender. Drain and then process for
6–7 seconds. Scrape down, then add the yoghurt,
lemon juice, oil, cumin, and salt to taste. Process
for a further 10 seconds to combine. Chill
overnight to thicken.

Serve with pitta bread or French bread as a
starter or lunch dish.

NOTE
Do not freeze.

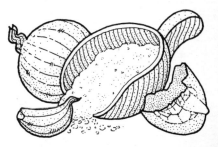

Stuffed Courgettes

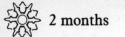 2 months

INGREDIENTS	Imperial	Metric	American
Courgettes	2 large	2 large	2 large
Cheese	2 oz	50 g	2 oz
Hard boiled egg	1	1	1
Ham	2 oz	50 g	2 oz
Fresh parsley	½ tsp	½ tsp	½ tsp
Salt and freshly ground black pepper			

Use the GRATING DISC. Cut the courgettes in half lengthways, scoop out the flesh, and leave to one side. Place the courgettes in an oven-proof dish. Grate the cheese, then remove from the bowl.

Fit the METAL BLADE. Chop the egg roughly for 2–3 seconds. Add the flesh of the courgettes, the ham cut into pieces, half the cheese, the parsley, salt and pepper. Process for 3–4 seconds until combined. Fill the courgette shells with this mixture and sprinkle the remaining cheese on top. Bake at 375°F/190°C/Gas mark 5 for 30 minutes.

Serve hot as a starter.

TO FREEZE
Freeze before baking. Thaw at room temperature for 3–4 hours, then bake as recipe.

SALADS AND SALAD DRESSINGS

How often in the interest of saving time do we put a piece of lettuce and a sliced tomato on the plate and call it salad instead of trying the more interesting and attractive options. With the processor on hand to do the time-consuming chopping and slicing, we can be more adventurous in our choice of salad recipes.

Mayonnaise and vinaigrette are probably the most popular salad dressings — there are simple and delicious recipes for both at the end of the following section.

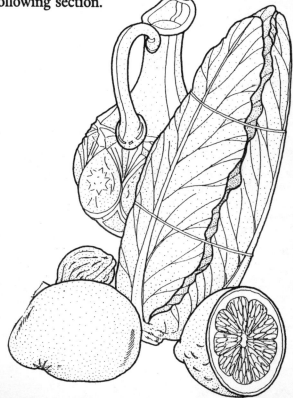

Coleslaw

INGREDIENTS	Imperial	Metric	American
White cabbage	1 lb	450 g	1 lb
Red eating apple	1	1	1
Carrots	3	3	3
Salad oil	6 tbsp	6 tbsp	6 tbsp
White wine vinegar	2 tbsp	2 tbsp	2 tbsp
Caraway seeds	1/2 tsp	1/2 tsp	1/2 tsp
Castor sugar	1/2 tsp	1/2 tsp	1/2 tsp
Salt and freshly ground black pepper			

1. Fit the SLICING DISC. Cut the white cabbage to fit the feed tube, removing the hard stalk. Slice and remove from the bowl.
2. Wash and quarter a red eating apple and remove the core. Slice through the slicing disc. Add to the cabbage.
3. Fit the GRATING DISC. Peel and trim the carrots and grate through the grating disc. Avoid forcing hard vegetables onto the grating disc, as this can cause some models to jam. Grating is slower than slicing. Add to the cabbage.
4. Fit the METAL or PLASTIC BLADE. Place the dressing ingredients in the processor, fitted with the metal or plastic blade.
5. Process until the dressing thickens. This usually only takes about 3–4 seconds.
6. Add the dressing to the other ingredients, tossing to make sure it is well incorporated. Add the dressing just before serving otherwise the salad will lose its crispness.

Lemon Fennel Salad

INGREDIENTS	Imperial	Metric	American
Fennel	*1 head*	*1 head*	*1 head*
Lemon	*1*	*1*	*1*
Salad oil	*2 tbsp*	*2 tbsp*	*2 tbsp*
Natural yoghurt	*2 tbsp*	*2 tbsp*	*2 tbsp*
Sugar	*2 tsp*	*2 tsp*	*2 tsp*
Salt and freshly ground black pepper			
Black olives	6	6	6

Use the SLICING DISC. Trim the top and base from the fennel and cut to fit the feed tube. Slice through the slicing disc and remove from the bowl. Cut half the lemon into thick slices and trim the peel away completely.

Fit the METAL BLADE. Place the lemon flesh in the processor and process for 4–5 seconds until finely chopped. Squeeze a tablespoon of juice from the other half of the lemon and add to processor. Add the oil, yoghurt and sugar and season with salt and pepper. Process for 6–7 seconds until thick. Toss the sliced fennel in this dressing and garnish with the black olives.

NOTE
Do not freeze.

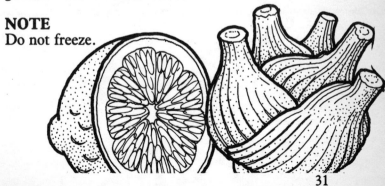

Waldorf Salad

INGREDIENTS	Imperial	Metric	American
Walnuts	2	2	2
Chinese leaf	½ head	½ head	½ head
Red eating apples	2	2	2
Lemon juice	2 tbsp	2 tbsp	2 tbsp
Salad oil	6 tbsp	6 tbsp	6 tbsp
White wine vinegar	3 tbsp	3 tbsp	3 tbsp
Castor sugar	1 tsp	1 tsp	1 tsp
Salt and freshly ground black pepper			

Use the METAL BLADE. Chop the walnuts roughly for 3–4 seconds. Remove from the bowl.

Fit the SLICING DISC. Slice the washed chinese leaf. Remove. Quarter and core the apples without peeling, and slice through the slicing disc. Remove and sprinkle with the lemon juice.

Place the oil, wine vinegar, castor sugar and salt and pepper in the processor and process for 8–10 seconds until thick and well blended.

Mix the chinese leaf, apples and walnuts together in a serving bowl and add the dressing just before serving.

NOTE
Do not freeze.

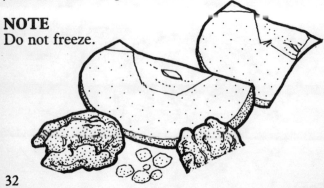

Avocado and Bacon Salad

INGREDIENTS	Imperial	Metric	American
Streaky bacon	6 slices	6 slices	6 slices
Avocado pears	2	2	2
Lemon juice	1 tbsp	1 tbsp	1 tbsp
Salad oil	2 tbsp	2 tbsp	2 tbsp
Salt and freshly ground black pepper			

Use the METAL BLADE. Derind the bacon and remove any eyes. Cut each slice into 4. Process for 3–4 seconds until finely chopped. Fry without extra fat until crisp.

Fit the SLICING DISC. Cut the avocados into 4, remove the stones and peel. Stand 2 quarters at a time in the feed tube and slice through the slicing disc. Remove and place in a shallow dish.

Fit the METAL BLADE. Scrape any mushy pieces of avocado from the lid and place in the bowl. Add the lemon juice, oil and salt and pepper and process for 5 seconds until thick. Pour over the avocado. Sprinkle the fried bacon pieces on top and chill before serving.

NOTE
Do not freeze.

Salad Nicoise

INGREDIENTS	Imperial	Metric	American
Tomatoes	8 oz	225 g	½ lb
Cooked potato	8 oz	225 g	½ lb
Cucumber	½	½	½
French beans	8 oz	225 g	½ lb
Canned tuna	4 oz	100 g	1 small can
Lemon juice	2 tsp	2 tsp	2 tsp
Black olives	8	8	8
Anchovies (optional)	1 small can	1 small can	1 small can

Use the SLICING DISC. Slice the tomatoes and use half to cover the base of a salad bowl. Reserve the rest. Slice the potato and remove from the bowl. Slice about a third of the cucumber and remove from the bowl.

Fit the GRATING DISC. Peel the remaining pieces of cucumber and grate. Cook the French beans for 5 minutes, drain and rinse under cold water. Cut into small pieces. Place the beans, grated cucumber, potato and the contents of the can of tuna, including the oil, in a mixing bowl. Mix well with a spoon, breaking up the tuna slightly. Add the lemon juice and stir, then place on top of the tomato slices in the salad bowl. Arrange the cucumber slices around the outside of the bowl, on top of the tuna mixture, and then arrange the remaining tomato slices in the centre. Garnish with the black olives and strips of anchovy. Chill well before serving.

Serve as a starter or lunch dish.

Les Crudités

INGREDIENTS	Imperial	Metric	American
White cabbage	¼ small	¼ small	¼ small
Celery	2 sticks	2 sticks	2 sticks
Carrots	8 oz	225 g	½ lb
Celeriac	½ medium	½ medium	½ medium
Cooked beetroot (beet)	8 oz	225 g	½ lb
Salad oil	6 tbsp	6 tbsp	6 tbsp
White wine vinegar	2 tbsp	2 tbsp	2 tbsp
Tarragon, dried	½ tsp	½ tsp	½ tsp
French mustard	½ tsp	½ tsp	½ tsp
Salt and freshly ground black pepper			

Use the SLICING DISC. Slice the white cabbage and place in a small serving dish. Slice the celery and place in a small serving dish.

Fit the GRATING DISC. Grate the carrots and place in a small serving dish. Peel the celeriac thickly, grate and place in a small serving dish. Grate the beetroot and place in a serving dish.

Wash the processor bowl and fit the METAL BLADE. Place the oil, vinegar, tarragon, mustard and salt and pepper in the bowl. Process for 10–12 seconds until the dressing thickens. Divide the dressing between the bowls of vegetables and chill for one hour.

Serve arranged on a tray with crusty wholemeal rolls or French bread.

NOTE
Do not freeze.

Mayonnaise

Good home made mayonnaise should be creamy yellow in colour and thick enough to spoon into a dish. It can take a lot of time and hard work to produce by hand. The processor will give perfect results with very little effort.

INGREDIENTS	Imperial	Metric	American
Garlic	1 clove	1 clove	1 clove
Egg yolks	3	3	3
Salt	½ tsp	½ tsp	½ tsp
English mustard powder	½ tsp	½ tsp	½ tsp
White wine vinegar	2 tbsp	2 tbsp	2 tbsp
Salad oil	½ pt	300 ml	1¼ cups
Lemon juice	1 tsp	1 tsp	1 tsp

1. Fit the METAL BLADE. Chop a clove of garlic (if used) into three, and drop onto the rotating blade through the feed tube to ensure it is finely chopped. Add the egg yolks, salt, mustard and about a third of the vinegar, and process for 3–4 seconds until combined.
2. With the motor running, add the oil in a thin steady stream, through the feed tube. Hold the jug an inch or two above the top of the feed tube. Choose a good quality oil such as olive oil, or safflower oil.
3. Once all the oil is incorporated, add the remaining vinegar and lemon juice to taste. The finished mayonnaise should be thick and glossy.

Green Mayonnaise

INGREDIENTS	Imperial	Metric	American
Fresh watercress	1 bunch	1 bunch	1 bunch
Fresh parsley	1 bunch	1 bunch	1 bunch
Garlic	1 clove	1 clove	1 clove
Salt	½ tsp	½ tsp	½ tsp
Egg yolks	3	3	3
English mustard powder	½ tsp	½ tsp	½ tsp
White wine vinegar	2 tbsp	2 tbsp	2 tbsp
Salad oil	½ pt	300 ml	1¼ cups
Lemon juice	1 tsp	1 tsp	1 tsp

Use the METAL BLADE. Wash the watercress and parsley and remove any hard stalks. Process for 10–15 seconds until finely chopped. Remove from the bowl. Have all the other ingredients at room temperature. Peel the clove of garlic, cut into 3 and drop onto the rotating blades to finely chop. Sprinkle in the salt, and add the egg yolks, mustard and 1 teaspoon of the wine vinegar. Process for 3–4 seconds. Then, with the motor running, pour the oil in through the feed tube in a very thin stream. Once the mayonnaise is really thick and all the oil is incorporated, add the remaining wine vinegar and the lemon juice and process for 3–4 seconds. Add the chopped watercress and parsley and process for 3–4 seconds to mix. Store in a screw-top jar or plastic box in a cool place but not in the refrigerator.

NOTE
This recipe may also be made with 2 eggs but the result is less thick and creamy. Use small bunches of watercress and parsley according to taste.
Do not freeze.

Walnut Vinaigrette

INGREDIENTS	Imperial	Metric	American
Walnut halves	6	6	6
Garlic (optional)	1 clove	1 clove	1 clove
White wine vinegar	1 tbsp	1 tbsp	1 tbsp
French mustard	½ tsp	½ tsp	½ tsp
Salt	¼ tsp	¼ tsp	¼ tsp
Salad oil	3 tbsp	3 tbsp	3 tbsp
Freshly ground black pepper			

Use the METAL BLADE. With the motor running, drop the walnut halves and garlic onto the blades and process for 7 seconds until the nuts are finely chopped. Stop the machine, scrape down the sides and add all the other ingredients. Process for 10 seconds until the sauce thickens. Store in a screw-top jar or a plastic beaker for up to a week.

NOTE
Do not freeze.

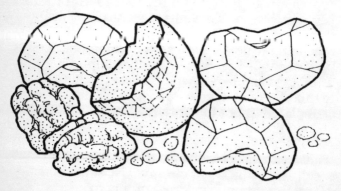

PASTRY

One of the most used techniques, pastry-making, can also be one of the most difficult skills to master.

Shortcrust pastry needs as little handling as possible to prevent the fat becoming soft and making the pastry heavy, the processor makes the pastry quickly with little or no handling, so results are consistently good.

Plain flour is best for shortcrust pastry. Wholewheat flour can also be used for savoury dishes, but should be mixed with self-raising flour. Different flours need different amounts of liquid, so add only two tablespoons of water, and then sprinkle in the remaining third, until the pastry begins to hold together.

Shortcrust pastry should always be covered and left to rest in a cool place, or in the fridge, for at least 30 minutes before rolling out. If this is not done the pastry will be difficult to roll and may shrink when it is cooked.

Choux pastry is easy to prepare and the finished dishes are attractive and popular. When making choux pastry it is important that the mixture remains firm and glossy. Eggs must therefore be added gradually to ensure that the pastry is stiff enough to hold its shape. Choux pastry is best eaten fresh and fillings should not be added far in advance, since this will tend to make the pastry soggy.

A biscuit base flan can be a quick and pleasant alternative to pastry for some sweet dishes. A recipe for this can be found at the end of this section.

Shortcrust Pastry

INGREDIENTS

	Imperial	Metric	American
Plain flour	8 oz	225 g	2 cups
Pinch of salt			
Butter or margarine	2 oz	50 g	1/4 cup
Lard	2 oz	50 g	1/4 cup
Water	2–3 tbsp	2–3 tbsp	2–3 tbsp

1. Fit the METAL BLADE. Place the flour and salt in the processor. Add the fat, cut into pieces. Using half white fat and half yellow gives the best texture and flavour.
2. Process until the fat is evenly cut up and mixed with the flour. This takes about 7–8 seconds.
3. The processed fat and flour should be smooth and free flowing, with no large lumps, and with no tendency to stick together.
4. Add the water through the feed tube with the motor running. Measure the water, and allow each tablespoon to be incorporated before adding the next spoonful.
5. Process until the mixture just forms a ball around the blade. Do not continue processing after this or the pastry will be overworked.
6. Turn out the dough, and pull together with the fingertips to make a smooth ball for rolling out.

NOTE: Shortcrust pastry can be used for both savoury and dessert dishes. A selection of recipes follows.

Bacon and Mushroom Quiche

4 months   Serves 4–6

INGREDIENTS	Imperial	Metric	American
Self-raising flour	3 oz	75 g	¾ cup
Wholemeal flour	3 oz	75 g	¾ cup
Pinch of salt			
Butter or margarine	2 oz	50 g	¼ cup
Lard	1 oz	25 g	2 tbsp
Water	2 tbsp	2 tbsp	2 tbsp
Onion	1 med	1 med	1 med
Oil	1 tbsp	1 tbsp	1 tbsp
Streaky bacon	6 oz	175 g	6 oz
Mushrooms	6 oz	175 g	6 oz
Milk	scant ¼ pt	150 ml	½ cup
Egg	1	1	1
Salt and freshly ground black pepper			
Caraway seeds	1 tsp	1 tsp	1 tsp

Use the METAL BLADE. Place the flours, salt and fats cut into pieces in the processor. Process for 7–8 seconds until the mixture looks like fine breadcrumbs. With the motor running, add the water through the feed tube until it just begins to form a ball around the blade. Remove, roll out and line a greased 9 inch/23 cm flan ring. Trim and peel the onion, cut into 4 and process for 3–4 seconds until roughly chopped. Fry in the oil until soft. Remove the rind and any eyes from the bacon and chop finely in the processor for 3 seconds. Remove. Add to the onion and fry for 2–3 minutes.

Fit the SLICING DISC. Wipe the mushrooms, slice and arrange in the flan ring. Sprinkle the bacon and onion on top. Beat the milk and egg, season, and pour into the flan. Sprinkle with caraway seeds and bake at 400°F/200°C/Gas mark 6 for 35–40 minutes.

Leek and Stilton Flan

✻ 3 months

INGREDIENTS	Imperial	Metric	American
Plain flour	3 oz	75 g	¾ cup
Wholemeal flour	3 oz	75 g	¾ cup
Butter or margarine	3 oz	75 g	⅓ cup
Stilton	2 oz	50 g	2 oz
Water	2 tbsp	2 tbsp	2 tbsp
Leeks	1 lb	450 g	1 lb
Butter	1 oz	25 g	2 tbsp
Streaky bacon	4 oz	100 g	¼ lb
Single (light) cream or milk	¼ pt	150 ml	⅔ cup
Eggs	2	2	2
English mustard	½ tsp	½ tsp	½ tsp
Salt and freshly ground black pepper			

Use the METAL BLADE. Place the flours, butter and
half the cheese in the processor and blend for
10 seconds until the mixture resembles fine
breadcrumbs. Add 2 tablespoons of cold water
through the feed tube with the motor running until
the mixture just forms into a ball. Remove and use
to line a greased 9 inch/23 cm flan ring.

Fit the SLICING DISC. Wash the leeks well and
remove the green tops. Slice. Melt the butter in a
saucepan, add the leeks and sweat over a gentle
heat for about 15 minutes until the leeks are soft.
Cool. Place the leeks in the pastry flan case.

Fit the METAL BLADE. Chop the bacon roughly
for 3–4 seconds. Sprinkle over the leeks. Mix the
milk or cream with the eggs and add the mustard,
and salt and pepper to taste. Pour this over the
leeks. Break the remaining Stilton into small
pieces and sprinkle over the filling. Bake at 400°F/
200°C/Gas mark 6 for 25–30 minutes. Serve hot
with salad.

Smoked Cheese and Vegetable Pie

✳ 2 months

INGREDIENTS	Imperial	Metric	American
Onion	1	1	1
Leeks	2	2	2
Oil	2 tbsp	2 tbsp	2 tbsp
Potato	1	1	1
	medium	medium	medium
Carrots	4	4	4
Sweetcorn (frozen or canned)	6 oz	175 g	6 oz
Smoked cheese	3 oz	75 g	3 oz
Eggs	2	2	2
Milk	6 tbsp	6 tbsp	6 tbsp
Salt and freshly ground black pepper			
Self-raising flour	4 oz	100 g	1 cup
Wholemeal flour	4 oz	100 g	1 cup
Butter or margarine	4 oz	100 g	½ cup
Mixed herbs	1 tsp	1 tsp	1 tsp
Water	3–4 tbsp	3–4 tbsp	3–4 tbsp

Use the SLICING DISC. Peel the onion, cut in half and slice in the processor. Wash and trim the leeks. Cut to fit the feed tube and slice. Heat the oil in a saucepan and sauté the onion and leeks for 5 minutes until soft. Meanwhile peel the potato, cut to fit the feed tube and slice. Arrange on the base of a pie dish.

Fit the GRATING DISC. Scrub and trim the carrots, put through the grating disc, then arrange on top of the potatoes. Add the sweetcorn to the pie dish and then add the leek and onion mixture.

Fit the SLICING DISC. Slice the smoked cheese using the slicing disc and arrange on top. Beat one of the eggs with milk, add the seasoning and pour over the vegetables.

Fit the METAL BLADE. Put the flours, butter and herbs in the processor and mix for 5–7 seconds. Gradually add the water until the mixture just forms a ball. Roll out the pastry and fit on the top of the pie dish. Trim the edges and decorate with pastry leaves. Glaze with beaten egg and bake at 425°F/220°C/Gas mark 7 for 20 minutes until the pastry is golden brown. Reduce the heat to 375°F/190°C/Gas mark 5 for a further 20–25 minutes.

Serve hot with noodles or salad.

TO FREEZE
Freeze the finished dish. Thaw at room temperature for 4–5 hours.

Onion and Pepper Tart

3 months

INGREDIENTS	Imperial	Metric	American
Cheese	2 oz	50 g	2 oz
Plain flour	6 oz	175 g	1½ cups
Pinch of salt			
Butter or margarine	3 oz	75 g	⅓ cup
Water	2 tbsp	2 tbsp	2 tbsp
Onions	2 large	2 large	2 large
Oil	1 tbsp	1 tbsp	1 tbsp
Red pepper	1 small	1 small	1 small
Eggs	2	2	2
Milk or single (light) cream	¼ pt	150 ml	⅔ cup
Salt and freshly ground black pepper			

Use the GRATING DISC. Grate the cheese, then remove from the bowl.

Fit the METAL or PLASTIC BLADE. Make the pastry. Place the flour and salt in the bowl, add the butter cut into pieces and process for 7–8 seconds until the mixture resembles fine breadcrumbs. Add the water through the feed tube with the motor running and process until the mixture forms a ball around the blade. Roll out the pastry and line a greased 8 inch/20 cm flan ring.

Fit the SLICING DISC. Peel and trim the onions and slice through the slicing disc. Fry in the oil until soft but not brown. Cut the pepper in half, remove the seeds and stalk and slice through the slicing disc. Add to the onions. Fry gently for 5 minutes. Mix the eggs and milk or cream together and season well. Place the pepper and onion mixture in the flan case and pour over the milk and eggs. Bake at 400°F/200°C/Gas mark 6 for 30–40 minutes until set and risen.

Cornish Pasties

6 months   Serves 6

INGREDIENTS	Imperial	Metric	American
Plain flour	8 oz	225 g	2 cups
Salt	1/4 tsp	1/4 tsp	1/4 tsp
Butter or margarine	2 oz	50 g	1/4 cup
Lard	2 oz	50 g	1/4 cup
Water	3–4 tbsp	3–4 tbsp	3–4 tbsp
Onion	1 small	1 small	1 small
Potato	1 medium	1 medium	1 medium
Carrot	1 medium	1 medium	1 medium

Stewing steak	8 oz	225 g	½ lb
Water	6 tsp	6 tsp	6 tsp
Worcestershire sauce	3 drops	3 drops	3 drops
Egg	1	1	1

Use the METAL or PLASTIC BLADE. Place the flour in the processor with the salt. Add the butter and lard cut into pieces. Process for 10 seconds until the mixture resembles fine breadcrumbs. With the motor running, gradually add the water until the mixture forms a ball around the blade. Divide the dough into 6 and roll each into a circle. Use a saucer to cut round to produce a neat circle about 6 ins/5 cm in diameter.

Use the METAL BLADE. Trim and peel the onion, cut into 4 and process for 3–4 seconds (or use the pulse button 3 or 4 times) until finely chopped. Remove from the bowl. Peel the potato and cut into 4. Peel the carrot and cut into 4. Place both in the processor and process for 4–5 seconds (or use the pulse button 4 or 5 times) until finely chopped. Remove from the bowl. Trim the fat from the meat, cut into cubes and process for about 8 seconds to mince the meat. Add the onions, carrots and potatoes and process for 3 seconds to mix the ingredients. Divide the mixture into 6, place on the centre of each pastry circle. Damp the edges of the pastry and fold the pastry over to make a half circle. Stand the pastie up and press most of the edges together leaving a gap of about 1 inch/2.5 cm at the top of each. Mix the water and Worcestershire sauce together and put a teaspoonful of this into each pastie. Seal the rest of the pastie, place on a greased baking tray and brush with beaten egg. Bake at 375°F/190°C/Gas mark 5 for 30–35 minutes.

TO FREEZE
Open freeze until hard, then pack in polythene
bags or boxes. Thaw at room temperature for
4 hours.

Chicken and Pork Layer Pie

2 months

INGREDIENTS	Imperial	Metric	American
Plain flour	10 oz	275 g	2½ cups
Pinch of salt			
Lard	1½ oz	40 g	3 tbsp
Butter or margarine	3 oz	75 g	⅓ cup
Eggs	2	2	2
Lean pork	12 oz	340 g	¾ lb
Onion	1 small	1 small	1 small
Belly pork	4 oz	100 g	¼ lb
Marjoram	½ tsp	½ tsp	½ tsp
Freshly ground black pepper			
Cooked chicken	4 oz	100 g	¼ lb

Use the METAL BLADE. Place the flour and salt in
the processor bowl. Cut the lard and butter into
pieces and add to the bowl. Reserve half an egg for
glazing and add the rest to the processor. Process
for 25 seconds until the mixture forms a ball
around the blade. Remove from the bowl. Cover
the pastry until needed.

Cut the lean pork into cubes and process in
short bursts, or use the pulse button until it is
finely and evenly chopped. It is best to process
only half the meat at a time. Remove from the
bowl. Peel the onion, trim and cut in quarters.

Process for 3–4 seconds. Remove from the bowl. Derind the belly of pork, remove any eyes and cut each slice into 4. Place in the processor and process for 7–8 seconds. Add the herbs, onion and pepper and mix for 3–4 seconds. Cut the cooked chicken into strips using a knife.

Divide the pastry into four and roll out into rectangles to fit the sides, base and top of a 1 lb/450 g loaf tin. Place a 1 inch/2.5 cm strip of greaseproof paper (double thickness) under the pastry along the length of the tin. Make it long enough to stick out either side and this will make it easier to turn out the pie. Place the side pieces in first, overlapping where they meet and moistening the pastry edges to seal. Position the base, overlapping with the sides to prevent the juices running out. Layer half the lean pork, then half the belly of pork mix in the base of the pie. Spread the chicken strips on top, then make a layer of belly pork and finish with a layer of lean pork. Put the pastry lid on and fold the side pieces over to seal the top. Pinch with finger and thumb around this double thickness of pastry to make a pattern. Decorate with pastry leaves. Glaze well with beaten egg and cut 3 steam vents in the top. Bake at 400°F/200°C/Gas mark 6 for 45 minutes. Lower the heat to 325°F/170°C/Gas mark 3 for a further 45 minutes. Allow to cool in the tin.

Serve cold, cut into slices.

TO FREEZE

Cool completely and slice. Interleave the slices with greaseproof. Wrap in foil or clingfilm. Thaw at room temperature for 3–4 hours.

SWEET RECIPES

Apple and Walnut Flan

6 months

INGREDIENTS	Imperial	Metric	American
Butter or margarine	*4 oz*	*100 g*	*½ cup*
Plain flour	*6 oz*	*175 g*	*1½ cups*
Castor sugar	*2 oz*	*50 g*	*¼ cup*
Egg yolk	*1*	*1*	*1*
Cold water	*1 tbsp*	*1 tbsp*	*1 tbsp*
For the filling			
Cooking apples	*1 lb*	*450 g*	*1 lb*
Walnuts	*1 oz*	*25 g*	*¼ cup*
Whipping (heavy) cream	*¼ pt*	*150 ml*	*⅔ cup*
Eggs	*2*	*2*	*2*
Castor sugar	*2 oz*	*50 g*	*¼ cup*
Cinnamon	*½ tsp*	*½ tsp*	*½ tsp*

Use the METAL BLADE. Cut the butter into pieces, and place in processor bowl. Add the flour and sugar and process for 10 seconds until the mixture resembles fine breadcrumbs. Mix the egg yolk and water and pour in through the feed tube with the motor running. Process for 8 seconds until the mixture just holds together. Turn out onto a lightly floured board or worktop and roll the pastry out. Line a 9 inch/23 cm flan ring. Chill the prepared flan ring while the filling is prepared.

Fit the SLICING DISC. Quarter the apples, remove the core and peel. Slice through the slicing disc then arrange in the flan case.

Fit the METAL BLADE. Chop the walnuts by processing for 5 seconds, then add the cream, eggs, castor sugar and cinnamon. Process for 5 seconds. Pour over the sliced apples. Bake at 400°F/200°C/Gas mark 6 for 10 minutes then reduce the heat to 325°F/180°C/Gas mark 3 for 30 minutes. Serve warm.

TO FREEZE
Open freeze until hard, then wrap in foil or clingfilm. Thaw at room temperature for 3–4 hours.

Crunchy Topped Apple Pie

3 months   Serves 4–6

INGREDIENTS	Imperial	Metric	American
Cooking apples	*1 lb*	*450 g*	*1 lb*
Orange juice	*2 tbsp*	*2 tbsp*	*2 tbsp*
Castor sugar	*1 tbsp*	*1 tbsp*	*1 tbsp*
Plain flour	*6 oz*	*175 g*	*1½ cups*
Salt	*¼ tsp*	*¼ tsp*	*¼ tsp*
Butter or margarine	*4 oz*	*100 g*	*½ cup*
Water	*2–3 tbsp*	*2–3 tbsp*	*2–3 tbsp*
Almonds	*1 oz*	*25 g*	*2 tbsp*
Honey	*1 tbsp*	*1 tbsp*	*1 tbsp*
Hot water	*1 tbsp*	*1 tbsp*	*1 tbsp*

Use the SLICING DISC. Quarter the apples, remove the cores, peel and slice through the slicing disc. Place in a pie dish, and sprinkle with the orange juice and castor sugar.

Fit the METAL BLADE. Place the flour and salt in the bowl, add the butter or margarine cut into pieces. Process for 8–10 seconds until the mixture resembles fine breadcrumbs. With the motor running, add the cold water through the feed tube until the mixture forms a ball around the blade. Roll out to fit the pie dish. Place the almonds in the processor and chop for 3–4 seconds (or use the pulse button 3 or 4 times). Add the honey and hot water, and process for 3 seconds until well mixed. Spread this mixture evenly over the pastry. Bake at 375°F/190°C/Gas mark 5 for 30–35 minutes until the top is crispy.

Serve hot with custard or Butterscotch Sauce.

TO FREEZE
Freeze before baking. Thaw at room temperature for 3–4 hours, then bake as recipe.

Creamy Banana Pie

INGREDIENTS	Imperial	Metric	American
Hazelnuts	*1 oz*	*25 g*	*¼ cup*
Plain flour	*4 oz*	*100 g*	*1 cup*
Butter or margarine	*3 oz*	*75 g*	*6 tbsp*
Castor sugar	*2 oz*	*50 g*	*¼ cup*
Water	*2 tbsp*	*2 tbsp*	*2 tbsp*
Custard powder	*1 oz*	*25 g*	*2 tbsp*
Castor sugar	*1 oz*	*25 g*	*2 tbsp*
Egg yolk	*1*	*1*	*1*
Milk	*¾ pt*	*425 ml*	*2 cups*
Whipping (heavy) cream	*2 tbsp*	*2 tbsp*	*2 tbsp*
Bananas	*2 large*	*2 large*	*2 large*
Chocolate	*1 oz*	*25 g*	*4 squares*

Use the METAL BLADE. Chop the hazelnuts for 10–12 seconds until finely chopped. Add the flour, the butter or margarine, cut into pieces, and 2 oz/50 g/¼ cup of castor sugar. Process for 6–7 seconds until the mixture is like fine breadcrumbs. Add 2 tablespoons of water through the feed tube and mix until the mixture just forms a ball around the blade. Roll out the pastry and line an 8 inch/20 cm flan ring. Prick the base with a fork and bake at 400°F/200°C/Gas mark 6 for 20–25 minutes. The flan should be just brown around the edges.

Place the custard powder, 1 oz/25 g/2 tbsp of castor sugar and the egg yolk in the processor. Add 3 tablespoons of milk and process for 7–8 seconds until smooth. Heat the rest of the milk and, when boiling, add to the processor and process for 4–5 seconds. Return to the pan and heat, stirring, until the sauce thickens. Return to the processor and process for 7–8 seconds, then add the cream through the feed tube with the motor running. Slice the bananas and place in the flan case. Pour the custard mix on top and leave to cool.

Fit the GRATING DISC. When cold, grate the chocolate through the grating disc and sprinkle over the pie.

NOTE
Do not freeze.

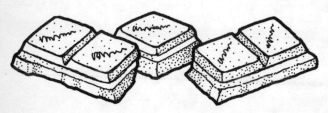

Walnut Bakewell with Pears

3 months

INGREDIENTS	Imperial	Metric	American
Plain flour	6 oz	175 g	1½ cups
Butter or margarine	3 oz	75 g	6 tbsp
Water	2–3 tbsp	2–3 tbsp	2–3 tbsp
Pears	2	2	2
Walnuts	2 oz	50 g	¼ cup
Self-raising flour	4 oz	100 g	1 cup
Soft (tub) margarine	4 oz	100 g	½ cup
Soft brown sugar	4 oz	100 g	½ cup
Eggs	2	2	2
Baking powder	1 tsp	1 tsp	1 tsp

Use the METAL BLADE. Place the plain flour and the butter or margarine cut into pieces in the processor and process for 7–8 seconds until like fine breadcrumbs. With the motor running add 2½–3 tablespoons of water and process until the mixture just forms a ball around the blade. Roll out the pastry and use to line a 9 inch/23 cm flan ring. Reserve the pastry trimmings.

Fit the SLICING DISC. Peel, quarter and core the pears, then slice. Arrange in the flan case.

Fit the METAL BLADE. Chop the walnuts finely. Add the self-raising flour, the soft margarine, the sugar, eggs and baking powder and process for 8–10 seconds until well combined. Spread the cake mixture over the pears, and re-roll the pastry trimmings into long strips to criss-cross the cake. Bake at 350°F/180°C/Gas mark 4 for 30–35 minutes, until well risen and brown.

Serve warm with cream or custard.

TO FREEZE
Freeze the finished dish, well wrapped in foil.
Thaw at room temperature for 3–4 hours.

Special Frangipan Tartlets

5 months   Makes 24

INGREDIENTS	Imperial	Metric	American
Plain flour	6 oz	175 g	1½ cups
Butter or margarine	3 oz	75 g	⅓ cup
Grated orange rind	2 tsp	2 tsp	2 tsp
Orange juice	2 tbsp	2 tbsp	3 tbsp
Butter or margarine	2 oz	50 g	¼ cup
Castor sugar	2 oz	50 g	¼ cup
Egg	1	1	1
Plain flour	1 oz	25 g	¼ cup
Ground almonds	1 oz	25 g	¼ cup
Icing (confectioner's) sugar	4 oz	100 g	½ cup
Water	3 tsp	3 tsp	3 tsp
Glacé cherries	6	6	6

Use the METAL BLADE. Place the flour and the
butter or margarine, cut into pieces, in the
processor. Add the orange rind and process for 3–4
seconds until the mixture resembles fine
breadcrumbs. With the motor running, add the
orange juice until the mixture forms a ball around
the blade. Roll out and cut with a 2 inch/5 cm
cutter and line 24 bun tins.

Place the butter or margarine, castor sugar,
egg, flour and ground almonds in the processor
and mix for 8–10 seconds until light and fluffy.

Divide the mixture between the pastry cases. Bake at 400°F/200°C/Gas mark 6 for 15 minutes. Allow to cool. Place the icing sugar in the processor. Add the water and mix for 5–6 seconds until smooth. Ice the cakes and decorate with sliced cherries.

TO FREEZE
Freeze before icing. Open freeze until hard, then pack in polythene bags. Thaw at room temperature for 2–3 hours, then ice as recipe.

Biscuit Flan Base

Biscuit based flans need no cooking when prepared in the processor. Digestive biscuits (Graham crackers) make a good base for many cheesecakes and fruit fools. Ginger biscuits go well with lemony flavours. Grated chocolate can be added to the biscuit base for a richer crust.

INGREDIENTS	Imperial	Metric	American
Digestive biscuits			
(Graham crackers)	*12*	*12*	*12*
Butter	*3 oz*	*75 g*	*6 tbsp*

1. Break up the biscuits roughly, and cut up the butter.
2. Fit the METAL BLADE. Process until finely chopped and mixed, but do not allow to stick together. This can take from 10 seconds to about 25 seconds.
3. Pour the mixture into a loose based flan ring and press down well with the hands.

Apricot Cheesecake

2 months   Serves 6

INGREDIENTS	Imperial	Metric	American
Digestive biscuits (Graham crackers)	12	12	12
Butter	3 oz	75 g	2/3 cup
Canned apricots	15 oz	425 g	1 large can
Gelatine	1 sachet	1 sachet	1 sachet
Cream cheese	4 oz	100 g	4 oz
Double or whipping (heavy) cream	1/4 pt	150 ml	2/3 cup
Flaked almonds	1 tbsp	1 tbsp	1 tbsp

Use the METAL BLADE. Break up the digestive biscuits and place them in the processor. Add the butter cut into pieces. Process for 15 seconds until well combined. Press into the base of an 8 inch/20 cm flan ring. Chill. Drain the apricots. Place 3 fl oz/85 ml/6 tbsp of the juice in a small bowl, sprinkle over the gelatine and place in a pan of warm water to dissolve. Reserve 2 apricot halves for decoration. Process the cream cheese for 15 seconds, then add the drained apricots and process for 10 seconds. Scrape down the sides of the bowl and add the cream. Process for 10 seconds. With the motor running pour the gelatine mixture in through the feed tube. Mix for a further 5 seconds. Pour on top of the biscuit base and chill for one hour. Decorate with flaked almonds, the apricot halves and extra cream if required.

TO FREEZE
Open freeze until hard, then wrap in polythene.

Choux Pastry

Making choux pastry by hand is hard work, as the eggs must be beaten in little by little for good results. The processor makes the job quick and easy, so profiteroles, eclairs and fancy gateaux can be made in minutes.

INGREDIENTS	Imperial	Metric	American
Flour	*4 oz*	*100 g*	*1 cup*
Pinch of salt			
Water	*7 fl oz*	*200 ml*	*scant 1 cup*
Butter or margarine	*3 oz*	*75 g*	*6 tbsp*
Eggs	*3*	*3*	*3*

1. Fit the METAL BLADE. Place the flour and salt in the processor.
2. Place the water and fat in a small pan and heat. Butter gives the best flavour, but other fats may be used.
3. As the fat melts, and the liquid rises up the pan, quickly add to the flour in the processor. Pour the liquid in through the feed tube with the motor running.
4. Once all the liquid is mixed in, add the eggs, one at a time, and process until the mixture is thick and glossy.
5. Place a piping bag, fitted with a plain tube, in a jug or jam jar and fold the top of the bag down. Spoon the mixture into this.
6. Fold the top of the bag over, and support the rest of the bag with the left hand. Pipe the choux pastry onto a baking tray, and bake as usual.

Profiteroles with Chocolate Sauce

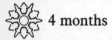 4 months

INGREDIENTS	Imperial	Metric	American
Butter or margarine	3 oz	75 g	6 tbsp
Water	7 fl oz	200 ml	scant cup
Plain flour	4 oz	100 g	1 cup
Eggs	3	3	3
Whipping (heavy) cream	1/4 pt	150 ml	2/3 cup
Chocolate	6 oz	175 ml	20 squares
Granulated sugar	4 oz	100 g	1/2 cup
Water	1/2 pt	300 ml	1 1/4 cups

Use the METAL BLADE. Place the butter in a small saucepan with 7 fl oz/200 ml/scant 1 cup of water and bring to the boil. Place the flour in the processor and start the motor. As the butter and water mixture begins to rise up the pan, pour the liquid in through the feed tube in a steady stream. Process for 10 seconds until smooth. Add the eggs one at a time with the motor running and process for a further 10 seconds until the mixture is smooth and glossy. Pipe or place teaspoons of the mixture onto lightly greased baking trays and bake at 425°F/220°C/Gas mark 7 for 12–15 minutes until well risen and golden. Remove from the oven and pierce the side of each profiterole to prevent it collapsing. Allow to cool. Open freeze if desired.

Whip the cream and pipe into the profiteroles.

Chop the chocolate in the processor for 10–12 seconds until finely chopped. Place in a pan with the sugar and 1/2 pt/300 ml/1 1/4 cups of water. Heat gently, stirring, then bring to boil and simmer for 10–15 minutes.

Pile the profiteroles into individual dishes and pour the chocolate sauce over.

MAIN MEALS

Many different meat dishes can be made much more quickly when using the processor. As you become more confident, try the more complicated dishes you might previously have avoided and enjoy experimenting with the many recipes that may be new to you.

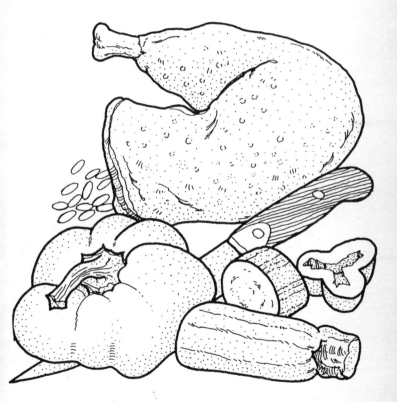

Rich Beef and Mushroom Cobbler

✳ 4 months

INGREDIENTS	Imperial	Metric	American
Onion	1 large	1 large	1 large
Garlic	1 clove	1 clove	1 clove
Oil	2 tbsp	2 tbsp	2 tbsp
Chuck steak	1 lb	450 g	1 lb
Mushrooms	4 oz	100 g	¼ lb
Plain flour	1 tbsp	1 tbsp	1 tbsp
Beef stock	¾ pt	425 ml	2 cups
Tomato purée (paste)	1 tbsp	1 tbsp	1 tbsp
Worcestershire sauce	1 tsp	1 tsp	1 tsp
Salt and freshly ground black pepper			
Juniper berries	4	4	4
For the topping			
Self-raising flour	8 oz	225 g	2 cups
Baking powder	1 tsp	1 tsp	1 tsp
Margarine	2 oz	50 g	⅔ cup
Mixed herbs	2 tsp	2 tsp	2 tsp
Milk	5 fl oz	150 ml	½ cup + 2 tbsp

Use the METAL BLADE. Peel the onion and cut into
4. Peel the garlic and cut into 4. Process for
3–4 seconds or use the pulse button 3 times to
chop evenly. Fry in the oil in a large pan. Cut the
beef into cubes and put half in the processor.
Process for 5–6 seconds until evenly chopped.
Remove, and repeat with the other half of the
meat. Add the meat to the onion and brown.

Fit the SLICING DISC. Wipe the mushrooms and slice through the slicing disc. Add to the meat and cook for 1 minute. Add the flour and stir in well. Pour in the stock and stir, then add the tomato purée, Worcestershire sauce, and salt and pepper to taste. Crush the juniper berries with a teaspoon and add to the meat. Bring to the boil, then simmer, stirring occasionally, for 15 minutes.

Fit the METAL BLADE. Put all the dry ingredients for the topping into the processor and mix for 3 seconds. Then, with the motor running, pour the milk through the feed tube until the mixture forms a soft dough. Pour the meat mixture into a casserole dish. Divide the dough into 8, roll into small balls and arrange around the edge of the casserole. Bake at 425°F/220°C/Gas mark 7 for 15–20 minutes.

TO FREEZE
Freeze the finished dish. Thaw at room temperature for 4–5 hours.

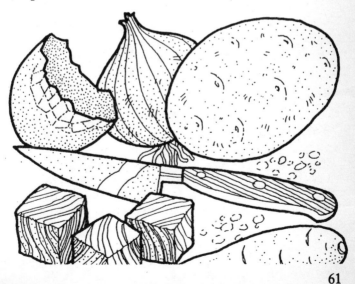

Homemade Hamburgers

6 months

INGREDIENTS

	Imperial	Metric	American
Bread	1 oz	25 g	1 slice
Stewing steak	1 lb	450 g	1 lb
Mushrooms	2 oz	50 g	2 oz
Thyme	1/2 tsp	1/2 tsp	1/2 tsp
French mustard	1/2 tsp	1/2 tsp	1/2 tsp
Salt and freshly ground black pepper			
Egg	1/2	1/2	1/2

Use the METAL BLADE. Make the bread into breadcrumbs by dropping it onto the rotating blades. Remove from the bowl. Cut the meat into cubes, trimming off any excess fat. Place the meat in the processor and process for 5–6 seconds until the meat is minced. Wipe the mushrooms, cut in half and add to the meat. Process for 4–5 seconds. Add the breadcrumbs, thyme, mustard and salt and pepper. Process for 2 seconds. Add the egg and process for 2–3 seconds. Tip the mixture onto a board and divide into 4. Shape into balls and then flatten into hamburgers. Grill or fry for 10 minutes, turning once.

Serve hot in seeded buns with salad.

TO FREEZE

Open freeze until hard, then stack in polythene bags or boxes. Thaw at room temperature for 3–4 hours.

Spaghetti Bolognese

6 months

INGREDIENTS

	Imperial	Metric	American
Onion	1	1	1
Garlic	1 clove	1 clove	1 clove
Oil	1 tbsp	1 tbsp	1 tbsp
Chuck steak	8 oz	225 g	½ lb
Mushrooms	2 oz	50 g	2 oz
Pigs' liver	4 oz	100 g	¼ lb
Sherry	1 tbsp	1 tbsp	1 tbsp
Plain flour	1 tbsp	1 tbsp	1 tbsp
Canned tomatoes	14 oz	400 g	1 large can
Beef stock	¾ pt	425 ml	2 cups
Tomato purée (paste)	1 tbsp	1 tbsp	1 tbsp
Oregano	2 tsp	2 tsp	2 tsp
Salt and freshly ground black pepper			
Spaghetti	8 oz	225 g	½ lb
Parmesan cheese			

Use the METAL BLADE. Peel and trim the onion and the garlic. Cut each into 4 and put into the processor. Use the pulse button or turn the machine on and off 3 or 4 times until onion and garlic are finely chopped. Heat the oil in a large pan and fry onion and garlic gently for 5 minutes. Trim the chuck steak, cut into cubes and process for 7–8 seconds in the processor until evenly minced. Add to the onions and brown, stirring continuously.

Fit the SLICING DISC. Slice the washed mushrooms. Add to the meat and cook for 2 minutes.

Fit the METAL BLADE. Chop the liver, trim and cut into 4, then process for 4–5 seconds. Add to the pan and stir well. Pour in the sherry and cook for 1 minute, then add the flour, stir, and pour in the tomatoes. Stir well to break them up and then add the stock, tomato purée, oregano, and salt and pepper to taste. Bring to the boil, then reduce the heat and cook, without a lid, for 20–30 minutes, stirring occasionally.

Meanwhile, boil the spaghetti in salted water as directed on the packet.

To serve, pour the sauce over the spaghetti and sprinkle with Parmesan cheese.

TO FREEZE
Pour the sauce into a plastic box. Thaw at room temperature for 4–5 hours or overnight.

Ravioli with Veal and Celery Stuffing

 2 months

INGREDIENTS	Imperial	Metric	American
For the pasta			
Eggs	2	2	2
Bread flour	8 oz	225 g	2 cups
Pinch of salt			
Water	2 tbsp	2 tbsp	2 tbsp
For the stuffing			
Onion	1 small	1 small	1 small
Garlic	1 small clove	1 small clove	1 small clove
Oil	1 tbsp	1 tbsp	1 tbsp
Lean veal	6 oz	175 g	6 oz
Celery	1 stick	1 stick	1 stick
Egg	½	½	½
Oregano	½ tsp	½ tsp	½ tsp
Salt and freshly ground black pepper			

Use the METAL BLADE. Place the eggs in the processor and process for 10 seconds. Weigh the flour out and tip onto a sheet of greaseproof paper, add the salt and then shoot the flour in through the feed tube with the motor running. Once all the flour is mixed, add the water and mix until the dough forms into a ball; add an extra teaspoon of water if needed. Run the machine for a further 35–40 seconds to knead the dough. Turn out, cover with a damp cloth and put aside for 30 minutes.

Meanwhile trim and peel the onion, and peel the garlic. Cut the garlic into 4 and drop through the feed tube with the motor running until finely chopped. Cut onion into 4, and chop finely in the processor for 3–4 seconds. Fry in the oil. Cut the meat into cubes and process for 6 seconds until finely chopped. Add to the onion and fry lightly. Wash the celery stick, cut into 4 and chop in the processor for 6–7 seconds. Remove the meat mixture from the heat, add the celery, egg, oregano, salt and pepper. Stir well.

Divide the dough into 2 and roll each piece out to a square about 16×16 ins/40×40 cm. Use plenty of flour to prevent the dough sticking. The dough should be very thin and you may have to stretch it lightly with the hands at the beginning. Place a teaspoon of the filling at about 1 inch/2.5 cm intervals on the sheet of dough. Moisten the dough in between the filling with a pastry brush dipped in water, and then carefully lay the other sheet of dough on top. Press the doughs together and cut with a sharp knife or a pastry wheel to make 16 little parcels. Cook in plenty of boiling water for 8–10 minutes. Serve hot with Parmesan cheese and mushroom sauce.

TO FREEZE
Open freeze until hard, then pack in a polythene bag. Thaw at room temperature for 3–4 hours.

Chicken Stuffed Pancakes

INGREDIENTS	Imperial	Metric	American
Plain flour	4 oz	100 g	1 cup
Egg	1	1	1
Milk	½ pt	300 ml	1¼ cups
Pinch of salt			
Oil	2 tbsp	2 tbsp	2 tbsp
Mushrooms	4 oz	100 g	¼ lb
Butter	3 oz	75 g	⅓ cup
Plain flour	1 oz	25 g	¼ cup
Chicken stock	½ pt	300 ml	1¼ cups
Mixed herbs	½ tsp	½ tsp	½ tsp
Salt and freshly ground black pepper			
Cooked chicken	8 oz	225 g	½ lb

Use the METAL BLADE. Place 4 oz/100 g/1 cup of flour, the egg, milk and salt in the processor and mix for 10 seconds until smooth. Use to make 8 pancakes, frying them in a little oil. Put aside.

Wipe the mushrooms and process for 3–4 seconds until roughly chopped. Fry in half the butter until soft, then add the flour, stir well and add the stock gradually. Bring to the boil, stirring continuously, and add the herbs and seasoning. Cut the chicken up roughly and process for 3–4 seconds until evenly chopped. Add to the sauce. Allow to cool.

Divide the sauce between the pancakes and fold the edges over to make square parcels. Place in a flat dish, folded sides down and distribute the remaining butter on top. Cover with foil and cook at 400°F/200°C/Gas mark 6 for 15–20 minutes until hot and golden.

Chicken and Ham Cannelloni

2 months

INGREDIENTS	Imperial	Metric	American
Onion	1 small	1 small	1 small
Cooked chicken	8 oz	225 g	1/2 lb
Mushrooms	2 oz	50 g	2 oz
Ham	2 oz	50 g	2 oz
Oregano	1 tsp	1 tsp	1 tsp
Salt and freshly ground black pepper			
Egg	1	1	1
Cannelloni	16 tubes	16 tubes	16 tubes
Butter or margarine	3 oz	75 g	6 tbsp
Plain flour	3 oz	75 g	3/4 cup
Milk	1 1/2 pt	900 ml	3 1/2 cups
Nutmeg	1/2 tsp	1/2 tsp	1/2 tsp
Cheese	2 oz	50 g	2 oz

Use the METAL BLADE. Peel and trim the onion and cut into 4. Place in the bowl and process for 4 seconds until finely chopped. Remove. Cut the chicken into cubes, place in the bowl and process for 6 seconds until evenly chopped. Remove. Wipe the mushrooms and place in the bowl. Add the roughly chopped ham. Process for 3 seconds. Add to the chicken. Add the oregano and salt and pepper. Beat the egg with a fork. Bind the mixture together with the egg. Stuff the cannelloni tubes with the mixture, and place in a shallow oven-proof dish. Put the butter, flour and half the milk in the processor and process for 8 seconds. Pour into a pan, add the rest of the milk, the nutmeg and salt and pepper. Bring to the boil, stirring continuously, until the sauce thickens. Pour over the cannelloni.

Fit the GRATING DISC. Grate the cheese and sprinkle over the sauce. Cook at 350°F/180°C/Gas mark 4 for 40 minutes. Serve hot with salad.

TO FREEZE
Wrap in foil before freezing. Thaw at room temperature for 3–4 hours.

Stuffed Pork Fillet

INGREDIENTS	Imperial	Metric	American
Prunes	9	9	9
Bread	*1 oz*	*25 g*	*1 slice*
Butter	*4 oz*	*100 g*	*½ cup*
Mixed herbs	*1 tsp*	*1 tsp*	*1 tsp*
Salt and freshly ground black pepper			
Pork fillet	*1½ lb*	*680 g*	*1½ lb*
Streaky bacon	*8 slices*	*8 slices*	*8 slices*

Use the METAL BLADE. Stone the prunes and place in the processor. Turn the machine on for 4 seconds to cut up the prunes, then drop the roughly cut bread through the feed tube to make breadcrumbs. Stop the machine and add 3 oz/75 g/⅓ cup of the butter, cut into pieces, the mixed herbs and salt and pepper. Process for 4–5 seconds until well mixed. Cut the pork fillets almost in half down the length, fill the centre with the stuffing mix, then fold the meat over again. Stretch the slices of bacon with a knife on a board, and then wrap the bacon around the meat. Cut the remaining 1 oz/25 g/2 tbsp of butter into pieces and put on top of the stuffed fillets. Grill under a hot grill for 15 minutes, turning once.

Serve with rice or pasta.

Braised Lemon Chicken

🌼 4 months

INGREDIENTS	Imperial	Metric	American
Celery	1 stick	1 stick	1 stick
Onion	1	1	1
Cooking apple	1	1	1
Butter	2 oz	50 g	1/4 cup
French mustard	1 tsp	1 tsp	1 tsp
Mixed herbs	1 tsp	1 tsp	1 tsp
Salt and freshly ground black pepper			
Lemon	1/2	1/2	1/2
Chicken portions	4	4	4
Chicken stock	1/2 pt	300 ml	1 1/4 cups

Use the SLICING DISC. Wash the celery and slice. Trim and peel the onion and slice. Peel, core and quarter the apple and slice. Place all the vegetables in the bottom of a casserole dish.

Fit the METAL BLADE. Place the butter, mustard, herbs and salt and pepper in the processor bowl. Add the grated rind and juice of half the lemon. Process for 6–7 seconds until soft. Make 2 slits across the top of each chicken portion and spread liberally with the lemon butter. Place the portions on top of the vegetables, add the stock and cover with a lid. Bake at 400°F/200°C/Gas mark 6 for 35–40 minutes. Remove lid for the last 10 minutes to allow the chicken to brown.

TO FREEZE
Cool completely and wrap in foil. Thaw at room temperature for 6–8 hours or overnight.

Chicken Roulade

INGREDIENTS	Imperial	Metric	American
Cheese	1 oz	25 g	1 oz
Plain flour	2 oz	50 g	1/2 cup
Butter or margarine	2 oz	50 g	1/4 cup
Milk	1/2 pt	300 ml	1 1/4 cups
Salt and freshly ground black pepper			
Eggs	2	2	2
Cooked chicken	4 oz	100 g	1/4 lb
Hard boiled egg	1	1	1
Milk	2 tbsp	2 tbsp	2 tbsp

Use the GRATING DISC. Grate the cheese, then remove from the bowl.

Fit the METAL BLADE. Place the flour, butter and milk in the processor and process for 10 seconds until well blended. Pour into a saucepan and heat, stirring continuously, until the sauce thickens. Season well. Return to the processor and process for 5–6 seconds. Remove 2 tablespoons of this mixture and set aside. Add the egg yolks to the sauce and process for 5–6 seconds until well blended. Whisk the egg whites in a large bowl until they form soft peaks. Add the sauce to the egg whites and lightly fold in. Grease a swiss roll tin and line with a sheet of greaseproof paper. Grease lightly. Pour the roulade into this and bake at 350°F/180°C/Gas mark 4 for about 15–20 minutes.

Chop the chicken roughly and process for 2–3 seconds until finely chopped. Add the hard boiled egg, cut into 4, and process for 2–3 seconds.

Place in a small saucepan along with the reserved sauce and 2 tablespoons of milk. Heat well, stirring. When the roulade is well risen and brown, turn out of the tin onto a sheet of greaseproof paper. Spread the sauce on top and roll up the roulade using the greaseproof to help roll it up. Place on an oven-proof serving dish, sprinkle with the cheese, and return to the oven for 5–10 minutes.

Serve hot with salad.

NOTE
Do not freeze.

Lamb Cutlets with Soubise Sauce

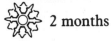 2 months

INGREDIENTS	Imperial	Metric	American
Bread	4 oz	100 g	4 slices
Mild onions	8 oz	225 g	½ lb
Water	¼ pt	150 ml	⅔ cup
Milk	¾ pt	425 ml	2 cups
Plain flour	1 oz	25 g	¼ cup
Butter or margarine	1 oz	25 g	2 tbsp
Salt and freshly ground black pepper			
Single (light) cream	1 tbsp	1 tbsp	1 tbsp
Egg	1	1	1
Lamb cutlets	8	8	8

Use the METAL BLADE. Drop the roughly broken bread onto the rotating blade to make breadcrumbs. Remove. Peel and trim the onions, cut into 4 and process for 3–4 seconds until finely chopped. Turn into a small pan, add the water and simmer for 10 minutes until soft.

Put the milk, flour and butter in the processor and process for 10 seconds until well blended. Pour into a pan and heat, stirring continuously, until the sauce thickens. Season. Put the onion and water in the processor and purée for 15 seconds until smooth. Add the sauce and cream and process for 4–5 seconds to mix. Beat the egg with 1 tsp of water and salt and pepper. Dip each cutlet in the egg and the breadcrumbs and then fry for about 10 minutes turning once.

Serve the cutlets with the sauce spooned around them, or serve the sauce in a jug with a spoon.

Lamb and Coriander Kebabs

✳ 2 months

INGREDIENTS

	Imperial	Metric	American
Scrag end of neck of lamb	*1½ lb*	*680 g*	*1½ lb*
Bread	*1 oz*	*25 g*	*1 slice*
Onion	*1*	*1*	*1*
Garlic	*1 clove*	*1 clove*	*1 clove*
Coriander	*3 tsp*	*3 tsp*	*3 tsp*
Rosemary	*½ tsp*	*½ tsp*	*½ tsp*
Butter	*2 oz*	*50 g*	*¼ cup*
Salt and freshly ground black pepper			
Green pepper	*1 small*	*1 small*	*1 small*
Boiling water	*1 pt*	*600 ml*	*2½ cups*
Tomatoes	*2 large*	*2 large*	*2 large*
Bay leaves	*4*	*4*	*4*
Oil	*1 tbsp*	*1 tbsp*	*1 tbsp*

Use the METAL BLADE. Remove the bone and the outside fat from the meat. Cut into cubes. Drop the bread in pieces through the feed tube onto the rotating blades to make breadcrumbs. Remove from the bowl. Peel and trim the onion and garlic and cut into 4. Place in processor with the coriander and rosemary. Process for 4–5 seconds, or use the pulse button 3 or 4 times, until the onion is finely chopped. Add the cubed meat and process for 8–10 seconds until it is minced. Add the breadcrumbs, the butter cut into pieces, and salt and freshly ground black pepper. Process for 4 seconds. Divide the mixture into 12 and shape into balls. Flour your hands to make this easier. Chill for 30 minutes.

Cut the pepper in half, remove the seeds and stem, and cut into strips at least ¼ inch/6 mm wide. Place in a dish, pour boiling water over and leave to stand for 2 minutes. Drain and rinse under cold water. Cut the tomatoes into 8 and remove the seeds. Arrange the lamb kebabs, tomato, green pepper and bay leaves on the kebab skewers. Brush the vegetables with a little oil, then grill for 15 minutes, turning once.

Serve with rice or hot pitta bread and salad.

NOTE
This recipe can also be made using 1 lb/450 g of cooked lamb, and is a useful way of using up leftover roast lamb.

TO FREEZE
Freeze the shaped kebabs in a rigid container without the vegetables. Thaw at room temperature for 2 hours before arranging the kebabs with the other ingredients on the skewers.

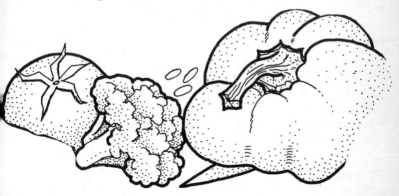

Moussaka

✳ 3 months

INGREDIENTS	Imperial	Metric	American
Cheese	2 oz	50 g	2 oz
Aubergines (egg plant)	2	2	2
Salt and freshly ground black pepper			
Onion	1	1	1
Garlic	1 clove	1 clove	1 clove
Cold cooked lamb	12 oz	340 g	¾ lb
Rosemary	½ tsp	½ tsp	½ tsp
Thyme	½ tsp	½ tsp	½ tsp
Tomato purée (paste)	2 tsp	2 tsp	2 tsp
Cornflour	1 tsp	1 tsp	1 tsp
Chicken stock	¼ pt	150 ml	⅔ cup
Milk	¾ pt	425 ml	2 cups
Butter or margarine	1 oz	25 g	2 tbsp
Plain flour	1 oz	25 g	¼ cup

Use the GRATING DISC. Grate the cheese and remove from the bowl.

Fit the SLICING DISC. Wipe the aubergines and cut in half. Slice through the slicing disc. Spread out on a plate, sprinkle with salt and leave.

Fit the METAL BLADE. Peel and trim the onion and cut into quarters. Peel the garlic and cut into 3. Drop the garlic onto the rotating blades to chop finely. Add the onion and chop for 3–4 seconds. Add the lamb, roughly cut up, and process for 10 seconds until well chopped. Add the herbs, tomato purée, cornflour, salt and pepper and process for 2–3 seconds to mix. Pour in the stock and mix again for 2–3 seconds. Place this mixture in a casserole dish.

Place the milk, butter and flour in the processor and mix for 10 seconds until well blended. Pour into a saucepan and heat, stirring, until the sauce thickens. Season well and add half the cheese. Drain the aubergines and place on top of the meat mixture. Pour the sauce on top and sprinkle the remaining cheese on top of this. Bake at 400°F/200°C/Gas mark 6 for 25–30 minutes.

TO FREEZE
Cover with foil before freezing. Thaw at room temperature for 4–5 hours.

Plaice Envelopes

INGREDIENTS	Imperial	Metric	American
Onion	1	1	1
Mushrooms	2 oz	50 g	2 oz
Butter	2 oz	50 g	1/4 cup
Salt and freshly ground black pepper			
Plaice fillets	4 small	4 small	4 small
Tomatoes	2	2	2

Use the METAL BLADE. Peel and trim the onion and cut into 4. Place in the processor and process for 3–4 seconds until finely chopped. Wipe the mushrooms and add to the bowl. Cut the butter into pieces and place in the processor. Season well and then process for 6 seconds.

Make a cut in the middle of each plaice fillet, through the flesh but not through the skin, along most of the length of the fish. Then make smaller cuts across the width of the fish at each end so that the flesh can be eased back from the middle of the fish to make a cavity. Divide the filling between the fish and then fold the flesh back over the filling slightly (it will not lay flat because of the stuffing). Slice the tomatoes and place 2 or 3 slices on top of each fish. Bake at 400°F/200°C/Gas mark 6 for 15–20 minutes, or fry in a large pan with a lid for 10 minutes.

Serve hot with rice or salad.

NOTE
Do not freeze.

SAUCES AND STUFFINGS

A good sauce can transform a meal, as all the best chefs know. Many people, however, hesitate to make their own sauces, because they believe them to be too difficult or time-consuming. The use of the processor can make sauce-making much more rewarding.

A good white sauce needs to be smooth and free from lumps. By mixing the flour, fat and milk in the processor before cooking, these ingredients can be well mixed and so the chances of lumps developing will be much less. Should any lumps still appear, simply whisk the sauce until it is smooth.

A number of different sauces can be made from a roux base — equal quantities of fat and flour cooked together with liquid added — for example the mushroom sauce recipe that follows. Simple sauces can also be made from a purée of vegetables — Tomato and Lentil sauce makes an ideal accompaniment for pasta and Cucumber Riata is delicious when served as a side dish with curry.

Parsley Sauce

INGREDIENTS	Imperial	Metric	American
Parsley	*1 bunch*	*1 bunch*	*1 bunch*
Milk	*¾ pt*	*425 ml*	*2 cups*
Flour	*1 oz*	*25 g*	*¼ cup*
Butter or margarine	*1 oz*	*25 g*	*2 tbsp*
Salt and freshly ground black pepper			

1. Fit the METAL BLADE. Place the washed parsley in the processor and chop finely. Remove from the bowl.
2. Place the milk, flour and fat in the processor. Process until the fat is finely chopped and the flour well mixed in.
3. Pour the mixture into a pan and heat, stirring continuously, until the sauce thickens.
4. When cooked, the sauce should coat the back of a wooden spoon.
5. Add the finely chopped parsley and season to taste.

Mushroom Sauce

✳ 4 months

INGREDIENTS	Imperial	Metric	American
Mushrooms	*2 oz*	*50 g*	*2 oz*
Oil	*1 tbsp*	*1 tbsp*	*1 tbsp*
Butter or margarine	*1 oz*	*25 g*	*2 tbsp*
Plain flour	*1 oz*	*25 g*	*¼ cup*
Chicken stock	*½ pt*	*300 ml*	*1¼ cups*
Tomato purée (paste)	*1 tbsp*	*1 tbsp*	*1 tbsp*

Salt and freshly ground
    black pepper

Use the METAL BLADE. Chop the mushrooms for 5 seconds until finely chopped. Fry in the oil. Mix the butter, flour, stock and tomato purée in the processor and process for 10 seconds. Pour on top of the fried mushrooms, bring to the boil, stirring continuously, and simmer for 15 minutes until well thickened. Season well.

Serve with ravioli or other pasta.

TO FREEZE
Cool and pour into a plastic box. Thaw at room temperature for 3–4 hours.

Tomato and Lentil Sauce

3 months

INGREDIENTS	Imperial	Metric	American
Lentils	*4 oz*	*100 g*	*½ cup*
Onion	*1*	*1*	*1*
Green pepper	*½*	*½*	*½*
Oil	*1 tbsp*	*1 tbsp*	*1 tbsp*
Canned tomatoes	*12 oz*	*340 g*	*1 large can*
Mixed herbs	*1 tsp*	*1 tsp*	*1 tsp*
Basil	*1 tsp*	*1 tsp*	*1 tsp*
Salt and freshly ground black pepper			

Use the SLICING DISC. Cook the lentils according to the instructions. Peel and trim the onion and slice through the slicing disc. Cut the pepper in half and remove the seeds and stalk. Slice through the slicing disc. Fry the onion and pepper in the oil until soft. Add the canned tomatoes and simmer for 10–15 minutes. Add the lentils and herbs and season well. Place in the processor and process for 10–15 seconds until smooth.

Serve with pasta.

Cucumber Riata

INGREDIENTS	Imperial	Metric	American
Cucumber	1/2	1/2	1/2
Natural yoghurt	1 small carton	1 small carton	1 small carton
Fresh chives	1 small bunch	1 small bunch	1 small bunch

Use the GRATING DISC. Peel the cucumber and cut to fit the feed tube. Grate the cucumber. Mix with the yoghurt. Sprinkle the chopped chives on the top.

Serve with curry as a side-dish.

NOTE
Do not freeze.

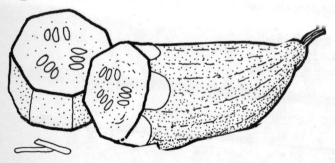

Sausagemeat

Made with fresh meats and no colourings or artificial flavouring, this can be frozen for up to 4 months.

INGREDIENTS	Imperial	Metric	American
Bread	1 oz	25 g	1 slice
Mixed herbs	1 tsp	1 tsp	1 tsp
Onion	1	1	1
Garlic	1 clove	1 clove	1 clove
Belly of pork	8 oz	225 g	½ lb
French mustard	1 tsp	1 tsp	1 tsp
Lemon juice	1 tbsp	1 tbsp	1 tbsp
Egg	1	1	1

1. Fit the METAL BLADE. Drop the bread, roughly broken up, and the herbs, through the feed tube with the motor running to make fine, even breadcrumbs. Remove from the bowl.
2. Cut the onion into quarters, and the garlic into 3 and process for 3–4 seconds until finely chopped. Use the pulse button if your machine has one, or turn the motor on and off several times to prevent overprocessing.
3. Trim the rind and eyes from the belly of pork, and cut each slice into 4. Add to the onions.
4. Process for 8–10 seconds until even in texture and colour and all the meat is chopped.
5. Add the herbs and breadcrumbs, the mustard and lemon juice, and then pour in the beaten egg through the feed tube.
6. The finished sausagemeat holds its shape well, and can be used for stuffings and sausage rolls.

Sausagemeat with Herbs

 3–4 months

INGREDIENTS	Imperial	Metric	American
Bread	1 oz	25 g	1 slice
Fresh parsley	1 large bunch	1 large bunch	1 large bunch
Fresh sage	2 leaves	2 leaves	2 leaves
Fresh thyme	2 sprigs	2 sprigs	2 sprigs
Onion	1	1	1
Garlic	1 clove	1 clove	1 clove
Belly of pork	8 oz	225 g	½ lb
Egg	1	1	1
Lemon juice	2 tsp	2 tsp	2 tsp
French mustard	½ tsp	½ tsp	½ tsp
Salt and freshly ground black pepper			

Use the METAL BLADE. Make breadcrumbs by dropping the bread onto the rotating blades. Add the herbs and process for 3–4 seconds until finely chopped. Remove from the bowl. Peel and trim the onion and garlic and cut into quarters. Process for 3–4 seconds until finely chopped. Remove from the bowl. Cut the rind from the belly of pork and cut each slice into 4. Place in the processor and process for 7–8 seconds until finely chopped. Add the onion and garlic, bread and herbs, egg, lemon juice, mustard and season well. Process for 5–6 seconds until well combined.

Use to stuff poultry and meat or for any recipe that requires sausagemeat.

TO FREEZE
Wrap in foil or clingfilm before freezing. Thaw at room temperature for 3–4 hours or overnight.

Stuffed Mushrooms

3 months

INGREDIENTS	Imperial	Metric	American
Flat field mushrooms	8	8	8
Onion	1	1	1
Garlic	1 clove	1 clove	1 clove
Bread	1 oz	25 g	1 slice
Fresh sage and thyme	1 tsp	1 tsp	1 tsp
Belly of pork	8 oz	225 g	½ lb
Egg	1	1	1
Lemon juice	1 tbsp	1 tbsp	1 tbsp
French mustard	1 tsp	1 tsp	1 tsp
Sherry	2 tbsp	2 tbsp	2 tbsp
Streaky bacon	2 slices	2 slices	2 slices

Use the METAL BLADE. Wash the mushrooms. Peel
and trim the onion and garlic and cut into 4. Put
both in the processor and process for 3–4 seconds
until evenly chopped. Remove. Drop the roughly
cut bread onto the blades with the motor running
to make breadcrumbs. Add the herbs and chop for
2 seconds. Remove the rind from the pork and cut
each slice into 4. Process for 8–10 seconds until of
even texture and colour. Add the breadcrumbs,
herbs, onion and garlic. Process for 3 seconds.
Add the egg, lemon juice and mustard and the
stalks of the mushrooms and process for 3 seconds.
Place the mushrooms white side down in a shallow
oven-proof dish. Divide the stuffing between the
mushrooms and pour the sherry around them.
Derind the bacon, chop roughly and process for 3
seconds until finely chopped. Sprinkle on top of
the mushrooms. Cover with foil and cook at
375°F/190°C/Gas mark 5 for 35 minutes.

TO FREEZE
Freeze cooked dish. Thaw at room temp. for 3-4 hours.

Apple and Walnut Stuffing

2–3 months

INGREDIENTS	Imperial	Metric	American
Bread	1 oz	25 g	1 slice
Walnuts	2 oz	50 g	½ cup
Onion	1	1	1
Eating apples	2	2	2
Fresh parsley	2–3 sprigs	2–3 sprigs	2–3 sprigs
Butter	1 oz	25 g	2 tbsp
Egg	1	1	1
Salt and freshly ground black pepper			

Use the METAL BLADE. Make breadcrumbs by dropping the roughly chopped bread onto the rotating blade. Remove from the bowl. Chop the walnuts for 3–4 seconds until roughly chopped. Remove from the bowl. Peel and trim the onion, cut into 4 and process for 2–3 seconds until roughly chopped. Peel, quarter and core the apples, cut into pieces and add to the processor. Process for 4–5 seconds. Add the breadcrumbs, parsley, the butter cut into pieces, walnuts, egg and season well. Process for 2–3 seconds to just combine the mixture.

TO FREEZE
Pack into a plastic box or polythene bag. Thaw at room temperature for 3–4 hours.

VEGETABLES

Liberated from the fiddly part of vegetable preparation, we can experiment with more elaborate vegetable dishes and can prepare interesting and inexpensive accompaniments to main meals.

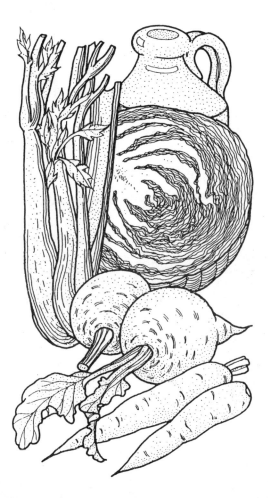

Braised Red Cabbage

✳ 6 months

INGREDIENTS	Imperial	Metric	American
Onion	1	1	1
Butter	1 oz	25 g	2 tbsp
Cooking apple	1	1	1
Red cabbage	1	1	1
	medium	medium	medium
White wine vinegar	2 tbsp	2 tbsp	2 tbsp
Water	3 tbsp	3 tbsp	3 tbsp
Sugar	2 tsp	2 tsp	2 tsp
Salt and freshly ground black pepper			

Use the SLICING DISC. Slice the onion and sauté in the butter. Slice the apple and add to the onion. Wash the cabbage, cut into segments to fit the feed tube and slice. This may need to be done in 2 or 3 batches depending on the size of the processor. Remove from the bowl. Place the apple and onion in the base of a casserole dish and add the cabbage. Mix the wine vinegar with 3 tablespoons of water, add the sugar and salt and pepper, then pour over cabbage. Put the lid on. Cook at 325°F/170°F/Gas mark 3 for 1½ hours.

TO FREEZE
Freeze the cooked dish.

Braised Celery Hearts with Orange

 1 month

INGREDIENTS

	Imperial	Metric	American
Onion	1	1	1
Butter	1 oz	25 g	2 tbsp
Carrot	1	1	1
Celery	2 hearts	2 hearts	2 hearts
Chicken stock	½ pt	300 ml	1¼ cups
Orange	1 small	1 small	1 small
Salt and freshly ground black pepper			

Use the METAL BLADE. Chop the onion for 3–4 seconds. Melt the butter in a pan and fry the onion until soft.

Fit the SLICING DISC. Slice the carrot, and then the celery. Add to the onion, stir well and then pour on the chicken stock. Add the juice and grated rind of the orange and season to taste. Pour into an oven-proof casserole with a tight fitting lid and cook at 325°F/170°C/Gas mark 3 for 1–1½ hours.

Serve hot. This is particularly good with lamb and pork.

TO FREEZE
Cool and pack into foil or plastic containers. Thaw at room temperature for 3–4 hours. Reheat at 375°F/190°C/Gas mark 5 for 20 minutes

Rosti

INGREDIENTS	Imperial	Metric	American
Potatoes	1 lb	450 g	1 lb
Salt and freshly ground black pepper			
Butter	1 oz	25 g	2 tbsp

Use the GRATING DISC. Peel the potatoes and cut to fit the feed tube. Cook in boiling salted water for 5 minutes only; the potatoes should still be hard. Drain and cool under running water. Grate the potatoes through the grating disc and season well. Melt the butter in a heavy pan and tip the grated potatoes in. Spread them out with a wooden spoon. Reduce the heat slightly and fry for 10 minutes. Have ready a flat plate the same size as the pan. Turn the potato mixture out onto this plate and then slide it back into the pan so that the other side browns. Cook for 5 minutes.

Serve hot, cut into wedges, with steaks and grills.

NOTE
Do not freeze.

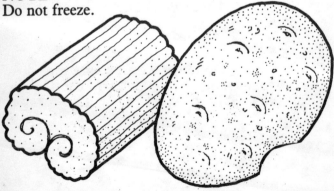

Sauté Potatoes with Peppers

INGREDIENTS	Imperial	Metric	American
Green pepper	*½*	*½*	*½*
Onion	*1 small*	*1 small*	*1 small*
Oil	*2 tbsp*	*2 tbsp*	*2 tbsp*
Potatoes	*1 lb*	*450 g*	*1 lb*
Salt and freshly ground black pepper			

Use the METAL BLADE. Remove the seeds and stalk from the pepper. Cut into 3 or 4 pieces. Trim and peel the onion and cut into 4. Place the pepper and onion in the processor and process for 3–4 seconds until finely chopped. Fry in the oil in a large heavy based frying pan for 4–5 minutes.

Fit the SLICING DISC. Peel the potatoes and slice through the slicing disc. Remove the onion and pepper from the frying pan and arrange the potato slices around the pan, overlapping slightly. Put the lid on and cook for 7–8 minutes until brown underneath and soft on top. Turn the potatoes over and sprinkle the pepper and onion on top. Season well. Cook for a further 5 minutes. Serve hot.

NOTE
Do not freeze.

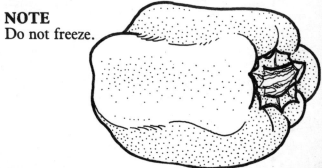

Stir Fried Vegetables

INGREDIENTS	Imperial	Metric	American
Leeks	2	2	2
Red pepper	1/2	1/2	1/2
Green pepper	1/2	1/2	1/2
White cabbage	small piece	small piece	small piece
Carrot	1 large	1 large	1 large
Salad oil			
Sherry	2 tbsp	2 tbsp	2 tbsp
Soy sauce	1/2 tsp	1/2 tsp	1/2 tsp
Salt and freshly ground black pepper			

Use the SLICING DISC. Wash and trim the leeks, slice, and remove from the bowl. Remove the seeds and stalk from the peppers and slice, then remove from the bowl. Slice the white cabbage and remove from the bowl.

Fit the GRATING DISC. Wash the carrot and grate. Have all the vegetables ready on small saucers or dishes, then heat a wok or large frying pan. Brush the base of the pan with a little salad oil before it heats up. Once hot add the leeks and cook, stirring continuously, for 2–3 minutes. Then add the peppers and cook, still stirring, for 2–3 minutes. Finally add the white cabbage and cook, stirring, for 1 minute. Mix the sherry and soy sauce together and season well. Pour this into the pan and stir the vegetables well to incorporate the sherry. Serve immediately.

NOTE
Do not freeze.

Celeriac au Gratin

2 months

INGREDIENTS	Imperial	Metric	American
Cheese	1 oz	25 g	1 oz
Celeriac	1 medium	1 medium	1 medium
Bread	1 oz	25 g	1 slice
Plain flour	1 oz	25 g	¼ cup
Butter or margarine	1 oz	25 g	2 tbsp
Milk	¾ pt	425 ml	2 cups
Salt and freshly ground black pepper			

Use the GRATING DISC. Grate the cheese, then set aside.

Fit the SLICING DISC. Peel the celeriac and cut to fit the feed tube. Slice through the slicing disc. Boil the slices of celeriac in salted water for 3–4 minutes only. Drain.

Fit the METAL BLADE. Drop the bread onto the blades with the motor running and continue to process to make fine breadcrumbs. Remove and set aside. Place the flour, butter and milk in the processor bowl. Process for 10 seconds until well blended. Pour into a pan and heat, stirring, until the sauce thickens. Add half the cheese and season well. Arrange the cooked celeriac slices in a casserole dish. Pour the sauce over and sprinkle the remaining cheese and the breadcrumbs on top. Bake at 375°F/190°C/Gas mark 5 for 15 minutes until golden brown. Serve hot.

TO FREEZE

Freeze in the dish covered with clingfilm. Thaw at room temperature for 3 hours. Reheat at 375°F/190°C/Gas mark 5 for 10–15 minutes.

Carrot and Lentil Purée

2–3 months

INGREDIENTS	Imperial	Metric	American
Lentils	4 oz	100 g	½ cup
Potato	1 medium	1 medium	1 medium
Carrots	8 oz	225 g	½ lb
Butter	1 oz	25 g	2 tbsp
Salt and freshly ground black pepper			
Single (light) cream	1 tbsp	1 tbsp	1 tbsp

Soak the lentils overnight, if necessary.

Use the SLICING DISC. Peel the potato and carrots and slice through the slicing disc. Cook in a little boiling salted water for 4–5 minutes until just soft. Drain well. Drain the lentils and place in a pan with just enough water to cover and simmer gently until soft and all the water is absorbed.

Fit the METAL BLADE. Place the lentils in the processor and purée. Add the carrots and potato slices, the butter cut into pieces, and salt and pepper. Purée until smooth. Add the cream through the feed tube and mix for 2–3 seconds.

Serve hot with roasts and grills.

TO FREEZE

Cool and pour into a plastic box. Thaw at room temperature for 5–6 hours. Reheat in a covered dish at 375°F/190°C/Gas mark 5 for 10–15 minutes.

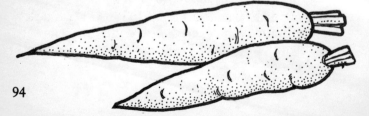

Ratatouille

✳ 3 months

INGREDIENTS

	Imperial	Metric	American
Aubergine (egg plant)	1 med	1 med	1 med
Garlic	1 clove	1 clove	1 clove
Onions	12 oz	375 g	¾ lb
Courgettes	8 oz	225 g	½ lb
Green pepper	1	1	1
Oil	2 tbsp	2 tbsp	2 tbsp
Canned tomatoes	14 oz	400 g	1 large can
Mixed herbs	½ tsp	½ tsp	½ tsp
Salt and freshly ground black pepper			

Use the SLICING DISC. Cut the aubergine to fit the feed tube and slice through the slicing disc. Place on a plate and sprinkle with salt. Leave for 30 minutes.

Fit the METAL BLADE. Peel the clove of garlic, cut into 3 and drop onto the blade with the motor running. Remove from the bowl.

Fit the SLICING DISC. Slice the onions and remove from the bowl. Slice the courgettes and remove. Cut the pepper in half, remove the seeds and stalk. Slice through the slicing disc. Fry the onion and garlic in the oil. Add the pepper and cook for 3–4 minutes until soft, then add the courgettes. Drain the liquid from the aubergines and add them to the pan. Add the tomatoes, mixed herbs and salt and pepper. Stir well. turn into a casserole dish and cook at 350°F/180°C/Gas mark 4 for 1½ hours.

Serve hot or cold as a first course or vegetable.

TO FREEZE
Cover the cooked dish with foil before freezing.
Thaw at room temperature for 3–4 hours.

Potatoes Anna

INGREDIENTS	Imperial	Metric	American
Potatoes	1 lb	450 g	1 lb
Butter	1 oz	25 g	2 tbsp
Milk	3 tbsp	3 tbsp	3 tbsp
Salt and freshly ground black pepper			

Use the SLICING DISC. Peel the potatoes and slice
through the slicing disc. Arrange in a casserole
dish in overlapping layers. About half-way
through, dot with half the butter. Finish with the
rest of the potatoes and the remaining butter. Add
salt and pepper to the milk and pour over the
potatoes. Cover with foil and bake at 375°F/190°C/
Gas mark 5 for 50–60 minutes.

NOTE
Do not freeze.

DESSERTS

Ice-cream, chocolate pudding, shortcake — all desserts, whether simple or more elaborate, can be prepared more quickly and very successfully in the processor — just wait for the compliments.

Orange and Banana Creams

INGREDIENTS	Imperial	Metric	American
Orange	*1*	*1*	*1*
Ripe bananas	*3 large*	*3 large*	*3 large*
Double (heavy) cream	*¼ pt*	*150 ml*	*⅔ cup*

Use the METAL BLADE. Remove the skin and pith of the orange with a sharp knife, cut it into four and process the flesh for 7–8 seconds until finely chopped. Add the bananas cut into pieces and process for 5–6 seconds until well mixed. Pour the cream in through the feed tube with the motor running and process for a further 5–6 seconds until thick. Pour into small dishes and chill before serving.

NOTE
Do not freeze.

Pear and Hazelnut Shortcake

1 month   Serves 8

INGREDIENTS

	Imperial	Metric	American
Hazelnuts	3 oz	75 g	¾ cup
Butter or margarine	4 oz	100 g	½ cup
Castor sugar	2 oz	50 g	¼ cup
Plain flour	5 oz	140 g	1¼ cups
Water	1 tbsp	1 tbsp	1 tbsp
Pears	2	2	2
Double or whipping (heavy) cream	¼ pt	150 ml	⅔ cup
Icing sugar	1 tbsp	1 tbsp	1 tbsp

Use the METAL BLADE. If the hazelnuts still have their brown skin on, remove this by warming the nuts in the oven and then rubbing them between your hands. Place the hazelnuts in the processor and grind for 10 seconds. Remove from the bowl. Mix the butter or margarine and sugar in the processor for 5 seconds, then add the nuts and flour. Mix for 5 seconds. Stop and scrape down the sides of the bowl. Mix again and add the water through the feed tube. Mix for 5 seconds. The mixture will not quite form a ball around the blade. Tip the mixture out onto a floured worktop and press it together with your hands. Divide into 2 and form a ball of each. Pat or roll each ball into a circle about / ins/18 cm diameter. The dough is crumbly but soft, so cracks can easily be smoothed away with the fingertips. Carefully place each circle on a greased baking sheet and bake at 375°F/190°C/Gas mark 5 for 10–12 minutes. The pastry should just brown around the edges. Cut 1 circle into 8 sections. Allow to cool on the trays.

Fit the SLICING DISC. Quarter the pears, peel and core each segment and slice through the slicing disc. Remove from the bowl.

Whisk the cream. Sieve the icing sugar over the pastry round that has been cut into segments. Place the other round on a serving plate. Spread about half the cream on top, then distribute the pears. Put the rest of the cream in a piping bag fitted with a large star nozzle and pipe 8 large rosettes on top of the pears. Lay each triangle of pastry on top of the rosettes of cream so that it rests at an angle. Eat within an hour of assembling.

NOTE
You can change the fruit according to season.

TO FREEZE
Open freeze the shortcake until hard, then remove to a biscuit tin or large plastic box. Thaw at room temperature for 4 hours before assembling and serving.

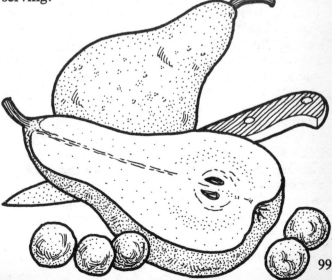

Chocolate Chip Ice-Cream

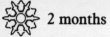 2 months

INGREDIENTS	Imperial	Metric	American
Chocolate	*2 oz*	*50 g*	*8 squares*
Eggs	*2*	*2*	*2*
Egg yolks	*2*	*2*	*2*
Castor sugar	*4 oz*	*100 g*	*½ cup*
Milk	*1 pt*	*600 ml*	*2½ cups*
Double (heavy) cream	*3 fl oz*	*85 ml*	*6 tbsp*

Use the METAL BLADE. Break up the chocolate and place in the processor. Process for 10–12 seconds until finely chopped. Remove from the bowl. Place the eggs, egg yolks and sugar in the processor and mix for 10 seconds. Heat the milk in a pan. With the motor running pour the warmed milk in through the feed tube. Pour the mixture back into the pan and heat, stirring, until the mixture coats the back of a wooden spoon. Pour into a tray and allow to cool. Place in the freezer for approximately 2 hours. When the ice-cream is set around the edges and just icy in the middle place it back in the processor and process for 8–10 seconds until smooth. Pour in the cream and mix for 8–10 seconds. Add the chocolate pieces and mix for 2 seconds to just mix. Return to the tray and freeze for 4–5 hours. Thaw for 20 minutes before serving.

NOTE
Vary the flavour of the ice-cream by using fruit purées or chopped nuts.

Rich Chocolate Pudding

INGREDIENTS	Imperial	Metric	American
Soft brown sugar	*4 oz*	*100 g*	*½ cup*
Self-raising flour	*4 oz*	*100 g*	*1 cup*
Baking powder	*1 tsp*	*1 tsp*	*1 tsp*
Cocoa powder	*1 oz*	*25 g*	*2 tbsp*
Butter or margarine	*4 oz*	*100 g*	*½ cup*
Eggs	*2*	*2*	*2*
For the sauce			
Cocoa powder	*1 tbsp*	*1 tbsp*	*1 tbsp*
Cornflour	*1 tsp*	*1 tsp*	*1 tsp*
Sugar	*2 tsp*	*2 tsp*	*2 tsp*
Water	*10 tbsp*	*10 tbsp*	*10 tbsp*

Use the METAL BLADE. Put the sugar, flour, baking powder and cocoa powder in the processor. Add the butter or margarine, cut into pieces, and the eggs and process for 8–10 seconds. Liberally butter the base of a 2 pt/1.1 litre casserole dish and turn the pudding mixture into this.

Place the cocoa powder, cornflour, sugar and water in the processor and mix for 4–5 seconds. Pour on top of the pudding mixture and leave to stand for 5 minutes. Bake at 375°F/190°C/Gas mark 5 for 40–45 minutes. Loosen the sides of pudding and turn out onto a serving dish. The pudding will be moist and soggy on the top with a crisper base.

Serve with cream or custard as it is very rich.

NOTE
Do not freeze.

Pineapple Sorbet

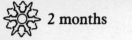 2 months

INGREDIENTS	Imperial	Metric	American
Canned pineaple	14 oz	400 g	1 large can
Granulated sugar	6 oz	175 g	¾ cup
Water			
Lemon	1	1	1
Egg white	1	1	1

Use the METAL BLADE. Drain the pineapple juice into a measuring jug. Make up to 1 pt/600 ml/ 2½ cups with water and add the sugar. Pour into a saucepan and heat gently so the sugar dissolves. Peel the lemon rind using a potato peeler, add these thin strips of lemon rind to the sugar solution and boil for 5 minutes. Add the lemon juice and leave to cool. Place the pineapple, roughly cut up, in the processor and process for 7–8 seconds until puréed. Add to the sugar syrup. Cool. Pour into a tray or casserole dish and freeze for 2 hours. When the sorbet is firm around the edges and slushy in the middle, pour into the processor and process for about 7–8 seconds until smooth. Whisk the egg white and add to the sorbet in the processor. Mix for 2–3 seconds until well mixed in. Freeze again and serve straight from the freezer.

NOTE

For special occasions use a fresh pineapple. Cut it in half and scoop out the flesh. Pile the finished sorbet into the pineapple shell and decorate with the fresh pineapple pieces.

CAKES, BISCUITS AND YEAST COOKERY

There is nothing nicer than a home-made cake and yet so often now we feel that we do not have the time to do our own baking and reach instead for mixes or ready-made cakes.

The traditional method of creaming the fat and sugar for a Victoria sandwich beats in plenty of air to make the cake rise. The development of soft margarine has made it possible to combine all the recipe ingredients together and produce good results. This method does, however, need the addition of baking powder to help the cake rise.

The smell of freshly baked bread cannot be beaten and making bread is fun and easy to do with the processor. Try using the basic dough recipe to make pizzas. For even more elaborate yeast cookery, make Orange Savarin and impress your dinner party guests.

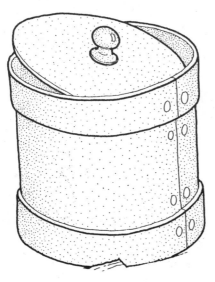

Victoria Sandwich

INGREDIENTS	Imperial	Metric	American
Self-raising flour	6 oz	175 g	1½ cups
Soft (tub) margarine	6 oz	175 g	¾ cup
Castor sugar	6 oz	175 g	¾ cup
Eggs	3	3	3
Baking powder	1 tsp	1 tsp	1 tsp

1. Fit the METAL BLADE. Place all the ingredients in the processor.
2. Process for 10–15 seconds, or until well blended.
3. Turn out the mixture into two sandwich tins and bake as usual.

Orange and Lemon Cake

4 months

INGREDIENTS	Imperial	Metric	American
Soft (tub) margarine	4 oz	100 g	½ cup
Self-raising flour	4 oz	100 g	1 cup
Castor sugar	4 oz	100 g	½ cup
Eggs	2	2	2
Orange	1	1	1
Lemon	1	1	1
Granulated sugar	1 tbsp	1 tbsp	1 tbsp

Use the METAL BLADE. Place the margarine, cut into pieces, in the processor. Add the flour, castor sugar and eggs. Process for 10 seconds until smooth. Grate the rind of the orange and add to the cake mixture along with 1 tablespoon of the juice. Mix for 3–4 seconds. Lightly butter an 8 inch/20 cm cake tin and turn the mixture into this. Grate the lemon rind and squeeze the juice. Mix the rind and juice with the granulated sugar and pour on top of the cake mixture. Bake at 350°F/180°C/Gas mark 4 for 35–40 minutes. Sprinkle with a little extra granulated sugar while still hot and allow to cool in the tin.

TO FREEZE
Wrap in foil or clingfilm before freezing. Thaw at room temperature for 4–5 hours.

Nut Cake

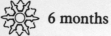 6 months

INGREDIENTS	Imperial	Metric	American
Nuts (walnuts, hazelnuts or almonds)	3 oz	75 g	¾ cup
Soft (tub) margarine	8 oz	225 g	1 cup
Self-raising flour	6 oz	175 g	1½ cups
Castor sugar	6 oz	175 g	¾ cup
Baking powder	1 tsp	1 tsp	1 tsp
Eggs	3	3	3

Use the METAL BLADE. Process the nuts for 15–20 seconds until finely ground. Add the margarine, flour, sugar, baking powder and eggs. Process for 12–15 seconds until well mixed. Place in an 8 inch/ 20 cm lightly greased cake tin and bake at 350°F/ 180°C/Gas mark 4 for 55 minutes. Allow to cool slightly in the tin before turning out.

This cake may be served plain, or iced with melted chocolate or glacé icing and decorated with whole nuts.

TO FREEZE

Cool and wrap in foil or polythene. Thaw at room temperature for 6–8 hours.

Quick Fruit Cake

4 months

INGREDIENTS

	Imperial	Metric	American
Self raising flour	8 oz	225 g	2 cups
Baking powder	1 tsp	1 tsp	1 tsp
Mixed spice	1 tsp	1 tsp	1 tsp
Castor sugar	4 oz	100 g	½ cup
Soft (tub) margarine	4 oz	100 g	½ cup
Eggs	2	2	2
Milk	5 tbsp	5 tbsp	½ cup
Mixed fruit	2 oz	50 g	½ cup
Glacé cherries	2 oz	50 g	½ cup
Demerara sugar	1 tbsp	1 tbsp	1 tbsp

Use the METAL or PLASTIC BLADE. Place the flour,
baking powder, mixed spice and sugar in the
processor. Add the margarine cut into pieces and
process for 10 seconds. Stop the machine and add
the eggs, milk, mixed fruit and whole glacé
cherries. Process again for 7–8 seconds until the
ingredients are just combined. Place in a greased
8 inch/20 cm cake tin and sprinkle the top with
demerara sugar. Bake at 350°F/180°C/Gas mark 4
for 50–60 minutes. Allow to cool slightly in the tin
before turning out.

TO FREEZE
Cool and wrap in foil or polythene. Thaw at room
temperature for 5 hours.

Butter Icing

The power of the processor makes butter icing very quick and easy. Make sure that the butter is at room temperature.

INGREDIENTS	Imperial	Metric	American
Icing (confectioner's)			
sugar	*6 oz*	*175 g*	*¾ cup*
Butter	*3 oz*	*75 g*	*6 tbsp*

1. Fit the METAL BLADE. Place the icing sugar and butter in the processor.
2. Process for 15–20 seconds until well blended. It may be necessary to stop and scrape down the sides of the bowl with a spatula. Add the colouring or flavouring through the feed tube with the motor running. A very small quantity of boiling water (about 1–2 teaspoons) will make piping the icing easier.
3. Turn out the icing and use as required. This icing will keep in the refrigerator and the freezer.

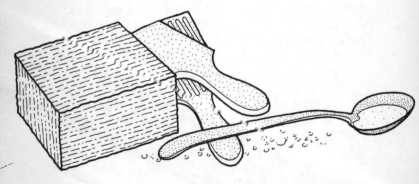

Chocolate Fingers

6 months   Makes 18–20

INGREDIENTS	Imperial	Metric	American
Eggs	2	2	2
Castor sugar	4 oz	100 g	½ cup
Self-raising flour	4 oz	100 g	1 cup
Soft (tub) margarine	4 oz	100 g	½ cup
Cooking chocolate	2 oz	50 g	2 oz
Golden syrup	1 tbsp	1 tbsp	1 tbsp
Icing (confectioner's) sugar	2 oz	50 g	¼ cup
Hot water	1–2 tbsp	1–2 tbsp	1–2 tbsp

Use the METAL BLADE. Place the eggs, sugar and
flour in the processor. Add the margarine, cut into
pieces, and process for 7–10 seconds until smooth.
Grease and flour a swiss roll tin and turn the
mixture into this. Bake at 350°F/180°C/Gas mark 4
for 15–20 minutes.

Melt the chocolate in a small dish over hot
water. Place the golden syrup, melted chocolate
and icing sugar in the processor and mix for 4–5
seconds. Add the hot water through the feed tube
with the motor running until the mixture is
smooth and thick. Spread the warm icing on the
cake and mark with a fork to make a pattern. Cut
the cake into fingers with a bread knife dipped in
hot water.

TO FREEZE
Open freeze until hard, then pack in polythene
bags or boxes. Thaw at room temperature for 3–4
hours.

Iced Walnut Biscuits

3 months   Makes 16

INGREDIENTS	Imperial	Metric	American
Walnuts	3 oz	75 g	3/4 cup
Butter or margarine	4 oz	100 g	1/2 cup
Brown sugar	3 oz	75 g	1/2 cup
Self-raising flour	6 oz	175 g	1 1/2 cups
Icing (confectioner's)			
sugar	2 oz	50 g	1/4 cup
Orange juice	1 tbsp	1 tbsp	1 tbsp

Use the METAL BLADE. Process the walnuts for 6 seconds until finely chopped. Add the butter, sugar and flour and process for about 20 seconds until the mixture forms a dough around the blade. Carefully remove and roll out the dough on a floured worktop. Use a fluted cutter to cut the biscuits, and re-roll the trimmings to make more biscuits. Bake at 350°F/180°C/Gas mark 4 for about 15 minutes. The biscuits should be an even brown when cooked. Allow to cool a little on the tray before moving to a cooling rack.

Fit the METAL BLADE to make the icing. Place the icing sugar in the processor and turn on the machine. Drip the tablespoon of orange juice through the feed tube onto the sugar. Stop and scrape down the sides of the bowl with a spatula and turn on again for 2 seconds (or use the pulse button once). Pipe the icing in lines over the biscuits, or use a teaspoon to trail the icing over the biscuits. Leave to set before serving.

TO FREEZE
Freeze before icing. Open freeze until hard, then pack into a plastic box. Thaw at room temperature for 3 hours. Then ice as recipe.

Basic Bread Dough

Most processors can only cope with small quantities of bread mixtures so do check in the instruction booklet. The initial mixing and kneading can be done in most processors, and often the knocking back of the risen dough can also be carried out in the processor.

INGREDIENTS	Imperial	Metric	American
Strong bread flour	8 oz	225 g	2 cups
Butter or margarine	1 oz	25 g	2 tbsp
Salt	1/2 tsp	1/2 tsp	1/2 tsp
Sugar	1/2 tsp	1/2 tsp	1/2 tsp
Fresh yeast	1/2 oz	15 g	1/2 oz
OR *Dried yeast*	1 tbsp	1 tbsp	1 tbsp
Milk	3 fl oz	85 ml	6 tbsp
Water	2 fl oz	50 ml	1/4 cup

1. Fit the METAL BLADE. Place the warmed flour and the salt in the processor and add the fat. Process for 4–5 seconds to rub in the fat.
2. If using fresh yeast place it in a jug with the sugar and mix with the back of a spoon until a creamy consistency is obtained. Then add the warmed milk and water. Dried yeast needs mixing with the sugar and milk and leaving in a warm place for about 20 minutes until it produces plenty of foam.

3. With the motor running add the milk and yeast mixture through the feed tube.
4. Once a dough is formed allow 20–30 seconds for the dough to be kneaded in the processor.
5. Turn the dough into a large bowl and cover with cling film or a damp cloth and stand in a warm place to prove. The dough is ready when it has doubled in bulk.
6. Return the dough to the processor and process for 10–15 seconds. This 'knocking back' ensures a fine, even texture in the finished bread. Shape the dough as required and leave to prove again in a warm place before cooking.

Individual Wholemeal Pizzas

3 months

INGREDIENTS	Imperial	Metric	American
Wholemeal bread flour	4 oz	100 g	1 cup
White bread flour	4 oz	100 g	1 cup
Salt	1/2 tsp	1/2 tsp	1/2 tsp
Butter or margarine	1 oz	25 g	2 tbsp
Fresh yeast	1/2 oz	15 g	1/2 oz
Sugar	1/2 tsp	1/2 tsp	1/2 tsp
Milk	3 fl oz	85 ml	3/8 cup
Water	2 fl oz	50 ml	1/4 cup
For the topping			
Onion	1	1	1
Red pepper	1 small	1 small	1 small
Cheese	4 oz	100 g	1/2 lb
Oil	1 tbsp	1 tbsp	1 tbsp
Oregano	1 tsp	1 tsp	1 tsp

Salt and freshly ground black pepper			
Tomatoes	*2 large*	*2 large*	*2 large*

Use the METAL BLADE. Put the flours in the processor with the salt and mix for 3 seconds to combine. Add the butter or margarine and mix for 3 seconds. Mix the yeast and sugar together using the back of a teaspoon to break the yeast up. Put the milk in a jug, add 2 fl oz/50 ml/¼ cup of boiling water, stir, then add the yeast and sugar. Stir well. With the motor running pour this liquid onto the flour and margarine until it forms a ball around the blade. Run the processor for 20 seconds to knead the dough. Place the dough in a bowl, cover with clingfilm and stand in a warm place to prove for 40 minutes, until the mixture has doubled in bulk. Turn the dough onto a floured worktop, divide into 4 and shape each into a ball. Roll out to circles about 6 ins/15 cm in diameter. Place on greased baking trays and put aside to prove while you prepare the topping.

Peel and trim the onion, cut into 4 and put in the processor and chop for 3–4 seconds. Remove from the bowl. Cut the pepper in half, remove the seeds and stem and chop roughly. Place in the processor and chop for 3–4 seconds. Remove from the bowl.

Fit the GRATING DISC. Grate the cheese. Brush each pizza round generously with oil. Divide the onion and pepper between the 4 rounds. Sprinkle the cheese over the top and then the oregano and salt and pepper to taste.

Fit the SLICING DISC. Cut the tomatoes in half and slice through the slicing disc. Arrange on top of the cheese. Bake at 400°F/200°C/Gas mark 6 for 20–25 minutes.

Serve hot with salad.

NOTE

Dried yeast can be used instead of fresh.
Substitute 1 teaspoon of dried yeast. Mix with the
warm milk and sugar in a jug. Leave to stand for
15–20 minutes until frothy. Add to the mixture
through the feed tube with the motor running.

You can vary pizza toppings according to
taste. Try smoked ham and tomato, bacon and
mushroom, or anchovy fillets and stuffed olives.

TO FREEZE

Open freeze the prepared pizzas before cooking,
then wrap each one in clingfilm. Cook from frozen
at 400°F/200°C/Gas mark 6 for 45 minutes.

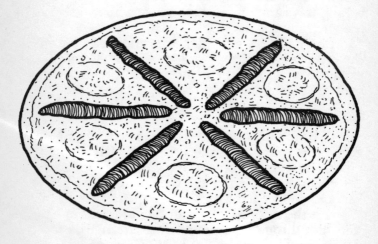

Orange Savarin

❄ 2 months   Serves 4–6

INGREDIENTS	Imperial	Metric	American
Bread flour	4 oz	100 g	1 cup
Milk	3 fl oz	85 ml	6 tbsp
Fresh yeast	1/2 oz	15 g	1/2 oz
Sugar	1/4 tsp	1/4 tsp	1/4 tsp
Eggs	2	2	2
Butter or margarine	2 1/2 oz	75 g	5 tbsp
For the sugar syrup			
Granulated sugar	4 oz	100 g	1/2 cup
Water	1/4 pt	150 ml	2/3 cup
Orange	1 large	1 large	1 large
Rum or brandy	2 tsp	2 tsp	2 tsp
Pink food colouring	2–3 drops	2–3 drops	2–3 drops
Double or whipping (heavy) cream	1/4 pt	150 ml	2/3 cup

Use the METAL BLADE. Warm the flour, place in the
processor and run the motor for 2–3 seconds to
sift. Warm the milk to hand hot. With the back of
a teaspoon, mix the yeast and sugar together until
it forms a paste, then pour on the milk. With
motor running pour this through the feed tube
onto the flour. Stop the machine. Break the eggs
into a jug, beat lightly and pour into the processor
through the feed tube with the motor running. Cut
the butter or margarine into several pieces and add
these one at a time, through the feed tube with the
motor running. Make sure each piece of butter is
well mixed before adding the next. Run the
machine for 10 seconds after the last piece has
been mixed in. Pour into an 8 inch/20 cm ring
mould or savarin mould. Cover with clingfilm or a

damp cloth and leave to rise for 45 minutes. Bake at 450°F/230°C/Gas mark 8 for 30 minutes.

Meanwhile make the sauce by dissolving the sugar in the water over a gentle heat. Use a potato peeler to remove 3–4 strips of orange rind from the orange and put these in the sugar syrup. Bring to the boil, boil for 1 minute, add the rum or brandy and remove from the heat. Colour the syrup with a few drops of pink food colouring. Turn the savarin out of the mould, (if it sticks, pour a little of the sauce onto the savarin around the edges). Pour the sauce over and leave to soak in.

Fit the SLICING DISC. Cut the orange into quarters, stand 1 quarter upright in the feed tube and slice. Remove the flesh from the remaining segments, cut each piece in half and use to fill the centre of a savarin. Arrange the sliced orange around the edge of the plate. Serve with cream.

NOTE
Dried yeast can be used instead of fresh. Substitute 1 tablespoon of dried yeast. Mix with the warm milk and sugar in a jug. Leave to stand for 15–20 minutes until frothy. Add to the mixture through the feed tube with the motor running.

TO FREEZE
Freeze before soaking the savarin with the sugar syrup. Open freeze until hard, then overwrap with foil. Thaw at room temperature for 2–3 hours.

PRESERVES

Peanut butter in twenty seconds and Almond Mincemeat in a fraction of the time it would normally take. If you thought life was too short to make your own chutney, you might be pleasantly surprised at how easily it can be made when you use the food processor.

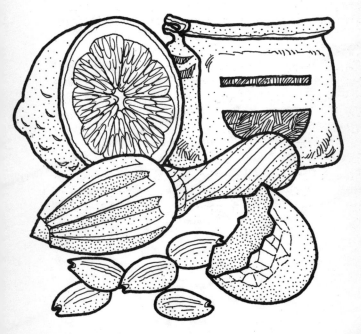

Almond Mincemeat

Makes 3–4 jars

INGREDIENTS	Imperial	Metric	American
Cooking apples	8 oz	225 g	½ lb
Almonds	1 oz	25 g	2 tbsp
Raisins	8 oz	225 g	½ lb
Currants	8 oz	225 g	½ lb
Sultanas	8 oz	225 g	½ lb
Mixed peel	4 oz	100 g	1 cup
Suet	8 oz	225 g	½ lb
Demerara sugar	6 oz	150 g	¾ cup
Sherry or brandy	3 tbsp	3 tbsp	3 tbsp
Lemon juice	2 tbsp	2 tbsp	2 tbsp

Use the SLICING DISC. Peel, quarter and core the apples. Slice through the slicing disc and remove from the bowl.

Fit the METAL BLADE. Chop the almonds for 8–10 seconds. Remove from the bowl. In a large bowl mix the dried fruits, mixed peel, suet and apple. Place about a quarter of this mixture in the processor and process for 10 seconds. Remove and process remaining quantity in batches. Mix the processed fruit and apple, sugar and almonds together and moisten with sherry or brandy and lemon juice. Stir well and pack into clean jam jars. Cover with jam pot covers. The alcohol ensures that this mincemeat keeps well.

Apple Chutney

INGREDIENTS	Imperial	Metric	American
Cooking apples	2 lb	900 g	2 lb
Sultanas	8 oz	200 g	½ lb
Onion	1	1	1
Lemon	1	1	1
Ground ginger	1 tsp	1 tsp	1 tsp
Vinegar	¾ pt	425 ml	2 cups
Caraway seeds	1 tsp	1 tsp	1 tsp
Soft brown sugar	1 lb	450 g	2½ cups

Use the METAL BLADE. Peel, core and quarter apples. Process in batches if necessary until very finely chopped. Remove and place in a large saucepan. Chop the sultanas for 10–12 seconds until finely chopped. Add to the pan. Peel, trim and quarter the onion and process for 5–6 seconds until finely chopped. Add to the pan. Add the grated rind and juice of the lemon, the ginger and half the vinegar and cook for 20 minutes until soft. Add the caraway seeds. Place the sugar and the remaining vinegar in the processor, blend for 4–5 seconds and then add to the pan. Cook until the mixture thickens. Pour into warm dry jars, and cover and pot as for jam.

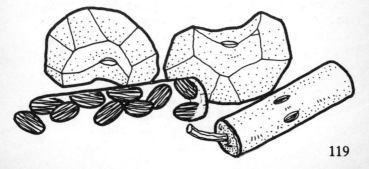

Peanut Butter

INGREDIENTS

	Imperial	Metric	American
Peanuts	8 oz	225 g	½ lb
Oil	2 tsp	2 tsp	2 tsp

Use the METAL BLADE. Process the peanuts for about 20 seconds until they form a paste. Scrape down, add the oil and process for a further 20 seconds. Store in a screw-top jar in the fridge.

Rum Butter

INGREDIENTS

	Imperial	Metric	American
Soft brown sugar	4 oz	100 g	½ cup
Butter	4 oz	100 g	½ cup
Rum	2 tsp	2 tsp	2 tsp

Use the METAL BLADE. Place the sugar in the processor. Add the butter, cut into pieces, and process for 10–15 seconds. Stop the machine, scrape down the sides and add the rum. Process for a further 10–15 seconds until soft and light. Store in small jars or tubs.

NOTE
Brandy butter can be made using castor sugar and brandy instead of brown sugar and rum.

Almond Paste

Makes enough for one 7 inch/18 cm cake

INGREDIENTS

	Imperial	Metric	American
Blanched almonds	8 oz	200 g	2 cups
Icing (confectioner's)			
sugar	6 oz	175 g	¾ cup
Castor sugar	6 oz	175 g	¾ cup
Egg	1	1	1
Lemon juice	2 tsp	2 tsp	2 tsp
Almond essence	2–3 drops	2–3 drops	2–3 drops

Use the METAL BLADE. Grind the nuts for 20–30 seconds until finely ground. Add the sugar, the egg, lemon juice and almond essence and process until the mixture forms a smooth ball. Wrap in clingfilm and chill before using.

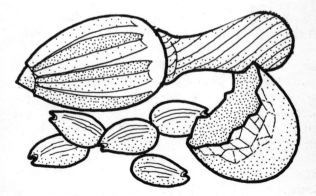

Three Fruit Marmalade

Makes about 4 jars

INGREDIENTS	Imperial	Metric	American
Grapefruit	2	2	2
Oranges	2	2	2
Lemons	2	2	2
Granulated sugar	2 lb	900 g	4 cups

Use the METAL BLADE. The fruit should weigh a
total of 2 lb/900 g. Cut the grapefruit into quarters
and remove the skin, pith and pips. Place the flesh
in the processor and process for 12–15 seconds
until finely chopped. Place in a preserving pan.
Cut the oranges into quarters, remove the pips and
remove the flesh from half of the segments and
process until finely chopped. Add to the
grapefruit.

Fit the SLICING DISC. Slice the remaining
orange segments, with the peel on, through the
slicing disc. Add to the preserving pan. Collect all
the pips and place in a small cotton or muslin bag
and place in the pan with the fruit.

Add 2 pints/1.1 l/5 cups of water and the juice
of the two lemons and bring to the boil. Simmer
for about 1 hour until the rind is soft.

Add the sugar and boil rapidly for several
minutes. Test for setting point by placing a
teaspoonful of the marmalade on a saucer and
allowing it to cool. If the surface wrinkles when
cool and the marmalade remains apart if a spoon is
dragged through the middle, it is ready to pot.
Remove from the heat and allow to stand for 10
minutes. Pour into clean warm jars, cover and
label.

INDEX

almond
  mincemeat 118
  paste 121
apple
  chutney 119
  pie, crunchy topped 50
  and walnut flan 49
  and walnut stuffing 86
apricot cheesecake 56
attachments 10
avocado
  and bacon salad 33
  and tuna mousse 26

baby foods 13
bacon
  and avocado salad 33
  and mushroom quiche 41
  and sweetcorn chowder 25
banana
  and orange creams 97
beef and mushroom cobbler,
  rich 60
biscuit flan base 55
braised
  celery hearts with
    orange 89
  lemon chicken 70
  red cabbage 88
bread
  basic dough 111
butter
  icing 108
  peanut 120
  rum 120

cabbage, braised red 88

cakes 103
carrot
  and lentil purée 94
  soup, velvety 21
cannelloni, chicken and
  ham 68
celeriac
  au gratin 93
  in crudités 35
celery hearts with orange,
  braised 89
cheese
  and vegetable pie,
    smoked 43
cheesecake, apricot 56
chicken
  and ham cannelloni 68
  lemon braised 70
  and mushroom pâté 23
  and pork layer pie 47
  roulade 71
  stuffed pancakes 67
chocolate
  chip ice-cream 100
  fingers 109
  pudding, rich 101
choux pastry 57
chutney, apple 119
cleaning 9
coleslaw 30
Cornish pasties 45
courgettes, stuffed 28
crudités 35
crunchy topped apple pie 50
cucumber riata 82

desserts 97

fennel and lemon salad 31
flan base, biscuit 55
frangipan tartlets, special 54
French onion soup 19
fruit cake, quick 107

grating disc 11
green mayonnaise 37

ham and chicken
   cannelloni 68
hamburgers, homemade 62
hazelnut and pear
   shortcake 98
hummus 27

ice-cream, chocolate chip 100
iced walnut biscuits 110
icing
   butter 108

lamb
   and coriander kebabs 74
   cutlets with soubise
      sauce 73
   moussaka 76
leeks
   and potato soup 18
   and Stilton flan 42
lemon
   fennel salad 31
   and orange cake 105
lentil
   and carrot purée 94
   and tomato sauce 81
loading the processor 8

mackerel pâté, smoked 24
main meals 59
marmalade, three fruit 112

mayonnaise 36
   green 37
metal blade 10
mincemeat, almond 118
moussaka 76
mushroom
   and bacon quiche 41
   and beef cobbler, rich 60
   and chicken pâté 23
   sauce 80
   stuffed 85

noise 12
nut cake 106

onion
   and pepper tart 44
   soup, French 19
orange
   and banana creams 97
   and lemon cake 105
   savarin 115
order of processing 8

parsley sauce 80
pasties, Cornish 45
pastry
   choux 57
   shortcrust 40
pâtés 22
peanut butter 120
pear and hazelnut
   shortcake 98
pepper
   and onion tart 44
   with sauté potatoes 91
pineapple sorbet 102
pizzas, individual
   wholemeal 112
plaice envelopes 78

pork
  and chicken layer pie 47
  fillet, stuffed 69
potato
  Anna 96
  and leek soup 18
  rosti 90
  sauté with peppers 91
preserves 117
profiteroles with chocolate
  sauce 58

ratatouille 95
ravioli with veal and celery
  stuffing 65
red cabbage, braised 88
rosti 90
roulade, chicken 71
rum butter 120

safety 9
salad nicoise 34
salads 29
sausagemeat 83
  with herbs 84
sauces 79
  mushroom 80
  parsley 80
  riata, cucumber 82
  tomato and lentil 81
sauté potatoes with
  pepper 91
savarin, orange 115
shortcake, pear and
  hazelnut 98
shortcrust pastry 40
slicing disc 10

smoked
  cheese and vegetable pie 43
  mackerel pâté 24
sorbet, pineapple 102
soubise sauce 73
soups 17
spaghetti Bolognese 63
starters 17-28
Stilton and leek flan 42
stir fried vegetables 92
storage 10
stuffed
  courgettes 28
  pork fillet 69
stuffings 79
sweetcorn and bacon
  chowder 25

timing 7
tomato and lentil sauce 81
tuna and avocado mousse 26

vegetables 87-96
  and smoked cheese pie 43
  stir fried 92
  soup, winter 20
velvety carrot soup 21
Victoria sandwich 104

Waldorf salad 32
walnut
  and apple flan 49
  and apple stuffing 86
  bakewell with pears 53
  biscuits, iced 110
  vinaigrette 38
whisk 12
winter vegetable soup 20

Opening
doors to
the World
of books

Book
Tokens

Book Tokens
can be
bought and
exchanged
at most
bookshops